SEA OF OKHOTSK

W9-BEZ-713

New
Siberian
Islands

LAPTEV
SEA

C E A N

Franz
Josef Land

80°

KARA SEA

Novaya
Zemlya

itsbergen

U S S R

70°

BARENTS SEA

NORWAY

90°
East

60°

SWEDEN FINLAND

miles
0   500
0   500
kilometres

ICEWALK

THE EXPEDITION

Patron
The Duke of Edinburgh's Award Scheme

Expedition Team
Robert Swan (*Leader* UK)   Dr Misha Malakhov (USSR)
Rupert Summerson (UK)   Darryl E. Roberts (USA)
Hiro Onishi (Japan)   Graeme Joy (Australia)
Arved Fuchs (West Germany)   Angus Kaanerk Cockney (Canada)

Advance Base Camp
Crispin Day (*Commander and Polar Team Reserve* – UK)
Stephen Williams (UK)   Keith Stanwyck (UK)   Dean Sassella (Australia)
Yoshi Ishikawa (Japan)

Resolute Liaison
John Tolson (*Camera* – UK)   Jeremy Morris (Australia)

Ottawa Headquarters
Jim Hargreaves (*Expedition and Logistics Manager* – UK)
Kirstie Hutchison (UK)   Lee Scott (Canada)
Christopher Holloway (Canada)   Christine McCabe (Australia)
Tracey Carpenter (Australia)   Jennifer Tomas (Canada)

Management and Administration
Richard Down (UK)   Wilfrid Grenville-Grey (UK)   Murray Fuller (UK)
Simon Dring (UK)   Lavinia Sidgwick (UK)   Kazuko Motegi (Japan)
Kirill Tchashin (USSR)   Bronwyn Bronz (Australia)   Casey Wondergem (USA)

ICEWALK

Robert Swan

With research and additional material by Christine McCabe,
Martyn Forrester and Dr Mikhail Malakhov

JONATHAN CAPE
LONDON

First published 1990
© Icewalk Features Ltd 1990
Jonathan Cape Ltd, 20 Vauxhall Bridge Road, London SW1V 2SA

Endpaper map © Malcolm Porter 1990

A CIP catalogue record for
this book is available from
the British Library

ISBN 0-224-02793-X

Typeset by Hope Services (Abingdon) Ltd
Printed in Italy by
New Interlitho SpA, Milan

AUTHOR'S NOTE

On 14th May 1989, eight men from seven nations stood at the North Pole. This book tells the story of their journey – a mere 56 days in a voyage which for some had begun more than one thousand days earlier. The untold Icewalk story is many times longer and far more complicated than the tale related here, involving as it does hundreds of individuals in several countries, many of whom gave more than three years of their lives to work tirelessly without pay.

Among those without whom this expedition would not have been possible I thank Rupert Summerson for being the finest deputy leader and travelling companion; Don Pratt of Barclays Bank in the Strand – surely the world's most patient bank manager; Jim Hargreaves, whose eleventh hour battle with Icewalk's mammoth logistical requirements guaranteed our success; Richard Down, for his administrative commitment and support; Kirstie Hutchison, who endured some of the worst office conditions imaginable; Lavinia Sidgwick, for ensuring that 22 students from 15 nations arrived in the High Arctic without mishap; and Leigh Anne Reynolds for producing a series of educational videos designed to take Icewalk to students worldwide.

I am indebted to our 'Headmaster', Dr Misha Malakhov, whose meticulous diary of the expedition helped bring a semblance of order to this book.

Above all, I thank Amway Japan Ltd whose generous sponsorship made Icewalk possible, and I commend the corporation's commitment to protecting our global environment – a commitment recognised recently by the United Nations Environment Programme. In particular I pay tribute to the personal assistance afforded this expedition by Amway at the most senior company level including the unstinting support of Rich De Vos, Jay Van Andel, Bill Nicholson, Bill Hemmer, Casey Wondergem and Peter Scacco.

ROBERT SWAN

Cumbria, England
11th January, 1990

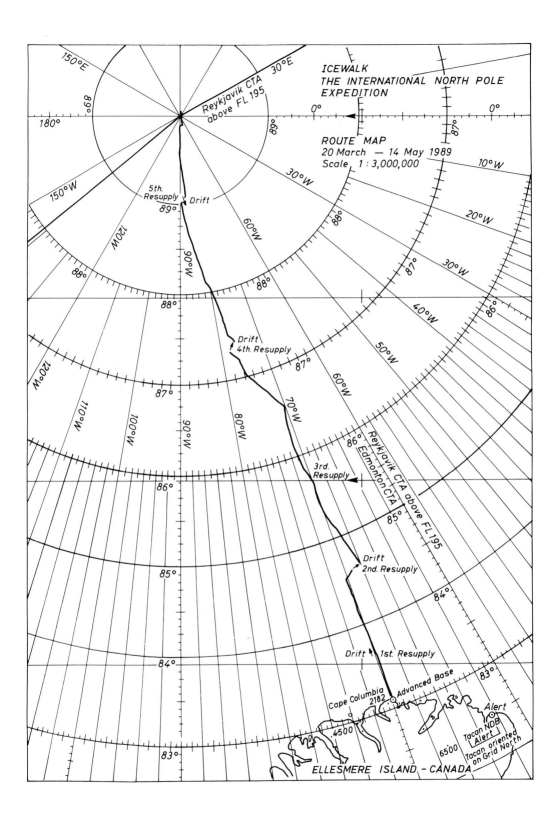

CONTENTS

Introduction: From the Jaws of Defeat   11
1   The Eighth Man   21
2   The End of the Beginning   31
3   Strangers in a Strange Land   45
4   The Sting of the Harness   55
5   Fire in the Tent   73
6   Through the Pain Barrier   91
7   Tigers and Dark Horses   102
8   The Great Unrest   123
9   A Fragile Bridge   140
10   War of Attrition   151
11   'Attack!'   169
12   Faces in the Ice   187
13   The Final Dash   198
14   The Pole   207
    Appendices   221
    Acknowledgments   241
    Bibliography   243
    Supporters and Sponsors   244
    Index   249

For Giles Kershaw, who died
tragically in Antarctica on 6th March, 1990.

1 'The attainment of the North Pole is, in my opinion, our manifest privilege and duty,' said American naval commander Robert E. Peary, whose claim to be first to reach the North Pole on 6th April 1909 is still the subject of controversy

Introduction

FROM THE JAWS OF DEFEAT

It was not an emergency, I kept telling myself, though our supplies of fuel were almost exhausted due to the second mysterious leakage in less than a week. As we sat huddled in the cold without stoves or food I realised that this was the very week in which, 77 years ago, Robert Falcon Scott had reported a fatal fuel shortage on his struggle back from the South Pole. It seemed that he was never far from me, even now, at the other end of the earth, crouched as we were in a small and vulnerable tent. Nearing absolute exhaustion, he had managed to scrawl: 'We have fuel to make two cups of tea apiece and bare food for two days . . . we shall stick it out to the end. We are getting weaker of course and the end cannot be far.'

As I followed in Scott's footsteps to the South Pole in 1986 I felt immense sadness. I was haunted by the images of his men. To look at those faces – the faces of his trusted companions – and know they were to die . . .

The radio crackled feebly, its bank of batteries emasculated by the knife-sharp cold. The ocean groaned beneath us, the ice pack creaking like a weary brigantine. I gazed round the tent at my seven weary friends. Darryl, with frostbite to his toes and inexplicable large blisters on his heels, was in obvious pain. Arved seemed to have aged half a century, his towering bulk shrivelled by a debilitating 'flu virus. Rupert had lost weight from his already slight frame; Hiro's cheeks were scorched with frostbite. Only Misha and Gus seemed at home in this most hostile of elements.

We had travelled only 37 nautical miles in seven days; there lay a further 377* between us and our goal. Radio contact with advance base camp at Cape Columbia had been patchy. It was minus 47 degrees celsius. We sat in silence each lost in his own thoughts. I felt a small

* One nautical mile is equal to 1.15 statute miles or 1.85 kilometres. See Appendix 1, page 221, on navigation.

knot of dread in my stomach. We could not travel further without fuel. So low were our provisions that we could not afford to eat full rations. The old South Pole adage, which I had bandied about so flippantly, came back to taunt me – 'No miles; no food'. If the weather worsened our resupply aircraft would be grounded in Eureka, unable to deliver more. We could be trapped for days. In these temperatures, that would be fatal.

It was one of the most difficult moments of my life. I did not have the skills or experience to navigate, or to break trail out on the ice, but as expedition leader I was ultimately – and publicly – responsible for the safety of the polar team.

I made up my mind quickly, before our disparate group had time to argue the matter through. I asked Graeme to 'crank up' the radio – an appropriate instruction, for the machine's laboured crackling and hissing conjured up visions of Indiana Jones-style adventure, not the technologically enhanced endeavour 'Icewalk' supposedly represented. Graeme blew into his cupped hands, an habitual rather than effective gesture, for his warm breath immediately froze. Painfully, he began to coax the radio to life.

We were to call for an immediate airdrop of essential provisions and remain camped until they arrived. It would have been foolish to jeopardise our chances at this early stage of the journey: six or seven gruelling weeks stretched before us, well beyond the hard blue horizon where sky became ice.

I rubbed my back slowly. I was aching and exhausted. I wondered if the others felt as tired as I did, if the realities of this undertaking gnawed also at their bones. This expedition was tough, far tougher than I had anticipated. It was colder than I had expected at this time of year, our path riddled with mountains of ice, and beneath us the ocean plotted countless treacheries. Perhaps we would not last beyond this first week. I had promised myself not to return without the Pole – but would a hero's death be as expedient as I imagined?

What in hell was I doing here?

✻

It began – if such a thing ever has a palpable beginning – in 1985, in a tiny hut on the tip of Cape Evans on Ross Island in Antarctica, as I sat hunched over an ancient typewriter in the depths of winter darkness, toying with the idea of a North Pole expedition. By 11th January, 1986, step one was completed. I stood at the South Pole with Roger Mear and Gareth Wood after manhauling 883 miles in 70 days. Success was

2 The loss of the *Southern Quest*

fleeting; some thousand miles away defeat was about to be snatched from the jaws of victory.

Southern Quest, the 550-ton former North Sea trawler that had been our home for so many weeks on the voyage to Antarctica, lay trapped off Beaufort Island. After a desperate struggle to free her, the crew of twenty-one huddled together in the cold and looked on as their ship was crushed by the worst pack ice seen in thirty years. A fire in the engine room had forced a swift evacuation of emergency equipment and provisions on to the ice. Helpless to do anything to save the stricken vessel, they watched her go in a few short minutes, swallowed by the ocean in a single gulp. The murderous ice floes were left stained red with paint from her hull as she went down. No one had been killed or injured, and tents, radios, food, rafts and navigation instruments had all been saved.

News of the loss reached me within minutes of our arrival at the South Pole, while we were still being greeted warmly by men operating in the domed American research station. It jerked me savagely back into the real world, for the sinking of the *Southern Quest* would play into the hands of those who wanted to prohibit private expeditions from Antarctica, an issue that had been hotly debated for some time. The expedition would now be portrayed as foolhardy and dangerous, implying (quite wrongly) that ultimately we were dependent on

government intervention and generosity.

   I had thought of this moment – of hoisting the Union Jack at the South Pole, of sitting in a chair and eating eggs and bacon – I had thought of this moment as signifying the end. Instead I knew I would have to begin again. I remember writing at the time: 'This might be when I find my best and turn disaster into something better.'

   Anything was better than a debt of half a million pounds (give or take the odd £50,000), a disgruntled and unpaid shipwrecked crew, and three of our men stranded in the Antarctic.

   I returned to England, my face peeling, my body 20 kilos lighter, haunted by ghosts from the past, sobered by the shadow of the future. Still dressed in our South Pole gear, Roger and I were thrust into a television studio where the glare of arc lights seemed more intense than the Antarctic sun. Many times we were asked the same questions – what was it like when staying alive had been our only concern, and should we have taken such risks in the first place? Our names appeared on the front pages and we watched our ship sinking on the six o'clock news. There were press conferences to answer the criticisms of us, which served only to magnify our baffling, dislocated feelings of victory and defeat, elation and depression, success and failure. But we were home. Family, green, trees, rivers, women, restaurants, friends, dancing – I had dreamed of them all, for more than a year.

The controversy generated by the loss of the *Southern Quest*, and the implications this posed for the future of private expeditions venturing into international territories, captured the media's attention for a very short time before the Footsteps of Scott Expedition was all but forgotten. With a simple flick of the media's remote control we faded into black.

As I elbowed my way through London's congested streets one evening soon after our return, a soft fog descending, I was suddenly overcome with an acute sense of loss. In the noise and the fumes of civilization, I realised that we had been cheated of the South Pole. Credit for a not insignificant 'first' journey – the first on foot to the Pole since Scott's epic of 1910–11, the first ever completely unsupported walk to the Pole manhauling every ounce of supplies every foot of the way – had been snatched from us unjustly in the very hour of triumph, and I wanted it back. At that moment, amid the bustle and roar of London, I knew that the journey to reclaim it was about to begin.

But where to begin? I had left the ship's crew lying on a beach somewhere in Australia, blown out by their three-year adventure. The *Southern Quest*'s captain, Graham Phippen, was working in Africa; although in no way his fault, the loss of the ship had been a severe blow to him, yet his support for us never wavered. Roger Mear had moved to the country to begin work on the book; Gareth Wood remained in the Antarctic with Steve Broni and Tim Lovejoy to clean up, for we were determined to leave the last unexploited wilderness as we had found it, with no trace of our presence.

While trudging South nine hours a day, for day after day, I had vowed never to walk anywhere again. Mentioning this to a friend as I contemplated a lecture tour to pay off some of our debts, I found myself despatched to the Mercedes dealer, Bradshaw & Webb, where I was presented with the keys to a brand new Mercedes Estate in honour of a destitute Polar explorer. I installed a car phone in my new portable office, and, in more style than I had dared to anticipate, started to pick up the pieces. With Annie Price, I established a base above a courier company in a derelict building in London's City Road, and with help from Kirstie Hutchison struggled to set up a lecture tour, to ward off debt collectors and to gear up some merchandising. We rationed the gas heating and sat at improvised desks, wrapped in anoraks and duvets when freezing winter came. We did everything ourselves, from booking

4 Robert delivers a dock-side lecture in London

venues to collecting money at the door. We slapped a 'Footsteps of Scott' lecture tour logo on the side of the Mercedes and, with Kirstie or Annie beside me, the back piled high with t-shirts and poster-size photos for sale, I began the punishing tour of Britain.

It was exhausting but exhilarating. To discover that so many people were far from indifferent to our story, our achievement, did much to restore my confidence. To come out of nowhere and have Sir Ranulph Fiennes jump to his feet to lead a standing ovation at the Royal Geographical Society; to speak before the Duke of Edinburgh; to return to my school at Sedbergh – these were indeed rewarding moments. Things did not always go so well, and I dreaded another cavernous hall like the one in Norwich where we had found an audience of four (including Kirstie's mother and an old 'Footsteps' hand) waiting to hear what I had to say.

As the money dribbled in, we paid off a little here, a little there, while at the same time trying to put aside enough to rescue Gareth and his two companions, still trapped in Antarctica. It seemed an over-whelming task, and without the unfailing support of the Expedition's bank manager, Don Pratt of Barclays in the Strand, it would have been impossible for a million lectures to have rescued me from financial ruin. Even so, those long motorway drives gave me time to think, and for those ideas of a journey North to germinate.

Time was pressing as 1986 drew to its close. We had to get Gareth, Steve and Tim out quickly, now that the sun had returned South. By February the long Polar night would be setting in again, and all hope of an evacuation would then have to wait another year. Besides, disturbing news of debilitation was appearing in the New Zealand press, soon to be taken up in London and New York papers. Our boys had asked no favours of the New Zealand and American bases in McMurdo, yet it seemed these nations were anxious to be rid of all traces of a 'Footsteps' presence.

It was Captain Giles Kershaw who finally came to the rescue. Giles, the most experienced Polar pilot that I knew, and our back-up in Antarctica a year before, contacted me with the offer of a Polar-equipped aircraft belonging to the Canadian-based company, Adventure Network, to bring the boys home; Dick Smith of *Australian Geographic* provided the funds. So it was that I found myself two weeks before Christmas rendezvousing with Giles in Punta Arenas. I arrived in Chile with little more than a serviceable brief case and a 'Don't Panic' badge. The latter Giles accepted as down payment and we took off in stormy weather for the 7,000-mile round flight across Antarctica in a tiny Twin Otter. The story of those extraordinary twenty-four hours in the air, a further ten on the ground refuelling, and of all that led to an

5 The Beardmore Glacier – Antarctica

emotional reunion with Gareth and his companions made a fitting epilogue to our book, *In the Footsteps of Scott.*

Two months later, the ship *Greenpeace* was able to penetrate the ice pack and anchor off Cape Evans, safely loading our hut, aircraft and all remaining food and equipment. By 11th February, 1987, nothing remained to show we had ever set foot on the Antarctic continent.

Strangely enough, it was while flying over the Antarctic in late 1986 that the essence of my new mission crystallised. As I gazed once again at the beauty of the wilderness, I recalled that Sir Ernest Shackleton had said Antarctica was 'the birthplace of the storm and the nesting place of the four winds'. Only from the air can the sheer sweep of the continent be appreciated and the truth of his description be understood. Long before, I had come to realise the importance of protecting Antarctica, the only continent not owned by anyone, the only continent to have escaped the ravages of war and imperial greed. Now, at the end of our Antarctic journey, I learned that this same continent had sadly not escaped the ravages of pollution. In 1985, a team led by Joseph Farman of the British Antarctic Survey had reported a 40 per cent loss in the ozone layer over Antarctica. We had unsuspectingly walked under that gaping hole; a hole which, it seems, grows larger year by year. By 1987 the average ozone concentration over the South Pole was depleted by 50 per cent, and in some isolated areas it had almost disappeared altogether during the spring. If we in the developed world continue to release industrial smoke, chlorofluorocarbons from spray cans and carbon dioxide from vehicle exhausts into the atmosphere at the present rate, it is but a matter of time before enough damage is done to cause ultra-violet rays from the sun to raise the average Polar temperature the 3° necessary to start an ice melt that could put London and New York under the sea.

The catalogue of environmental damage in Antarctica does not stop there. Huge mounds of non-degradable rubbish have piled up round some Antarctic bases. Penguins and marine life have been found to contain unacceptably high traces of toxic materials. In 1991, when the Antarctic Treaty which maintains the continent's international status is due to be renegotiated, we could see an end to the present ban on indiscriminate exploitation of minerals and oil in the region.

If a North Pole Expedition was to have a wider context, I decided, than merely that of Robert Swan attempting to become the first person in history to have walked to both Poles, north and south, in the 80th year after the American Robert Peary first reached farthest north, then it was essential to arouse youth to these environmental issues. With no quarter of the earth now left entirely unexplored, it seemed to me important to rekindle interest among students in our planet and to show by example that high adventure was still at hand, that quite ordinary people without advanced skills can realise the most astonishing and ambitious of goals if they set their minds to it. For only with the vision and courage of the old-time explorers are we going to solve the enormous geographical problems that threaten our well-being in the century to come.

My mind was made up: I would lead an international team, backed up by a party of young students, to the North Pole in 1989.

1

THE EIGHTH MAN

Without another dream to sustain me, the months following my return to England from the South Pole would have been unbearably depressing. The elation of success, of becoming the first (with my companions Roger Mear and Gareth Wood) to walk Scott's route to the Pole unaided by pre-laid depots or supply drops, had lasted a few short minutes. After that everything had come swiftly tumbling down. We had lost the political game (one not of our choosing); we had lost our ship and all financial credibility. Three men had remained behind, had given another year of their lives, in order to salvage what they could of our good name and our tattered belongings in and around the hut – within sight of Scott's own headquarters – at Cape Evans. I had no home to go to, no office, no assets of any kind beyond £100 or so in bank notes in my pocket. The scale of the debt the expedition faced was almost unthinkable, and before I had time to start thinking about it I decided to telephone a friend who was on board ship somewhere in the Bay of Biscay.

Rupert Summerson was returning home at the end of a three-year tour of duty with the British Antarctic Survey. I had met him aboard the RRS *John Biscoe*, where we had shared a cabin on our way to Antarctica in 1980. It was my first tour with the Survey, in which I was to serve (some thought appropriately) as Base General Assistant. Rupert held a Field post. We discovered that we had been to school together at the age of six in County Durham. Later he had made concerted if inconsistent efforts to seduce my sister. Our friendship endured even a circumnavigation together of Iceland's Vatnajokull ice-cap (the largest glacier in Europe) as part of my training for the South Pole venture. That had been as close to true *Boy's Own* adventure as I have ever come – no fund raising, no lectures, and no debts.

6 A bleak outlook at Cape Columbia

The crackling phone link was appalling. 'Look', I said to Rupert when finally we were connected, 'I'm giving a lecture to the Royal Geographical Society on the day you arrive. You ought to be there.'

'Why?' he asked. 'What's the rush?'

'I'm going to the North Pole,' I said with some abandon. 'If you want to come along, there is a place for you. You don't have to decide now, but think about it. I just want you to know there is a place for you.'

Rupert did not think about it. 'No, no! I don't need to decide. I'm coming,' he shouted.

And that was that. I had my first team member, a navigator. There was no money, and even the remote prospect of gaining sponsorship from my South Pole benefactor, Sir Jack Hayward, went flat when the freak October gale of 1987 demolished most of the ancient trees on his estate two days after the worst stock market crash since 1929.

By that time, the expedition headquarters had moved to Australia, where lectures tended to pull in more money than in Britain. Even so, it made little impression on the outstanding debt and none at all on my plans for the North, which I announced as if it were in the bag. 'If you are physically tough, articulate and would like to spend 66 days walking 965 kilometres in freezing conditions, Robert Swan would like to talk to you,' the *Sydney Morning Herald* reported. The *Daily News* called for '. . . one Aussie to drag a 180 kg sled over 1550 km of floating sea ice to the North Pole. The person must be fit, able to handle temperatures as

7 Ex-Royal Marine, Rupert Summerson, became Icewalk's navigator and
   deputy leader

8 Graeme Joy, Australian school teacher and champion kayaker

low as minus 50 degrees, be able to navigate and get on extremely well with three other team members . . . The applicant must also be a good public speaker who can communicate well with young people . . .'

What the papers did not say, and could not know, was that the applicant must also be resourceful, must work without remuneration for almost two years, and be prepared to abandon career, family, and home in the quest for an unmarked spot on a frozen sheet of ocean. The expedition, which one month earlier had been just an idea, took root in Australia with surprising alacrity. I asked Christine Gee to become the project's co-ordinator, and support began to come in almost immediately.

Graeme Joy, a Melbourne school teacher and champion canoeist, was among the first to ask to join us. When he approached me at one of my lectures, I displayed only vague interest with a weary request for him to 'put it in writing'. His letter turned up as one of hundreds in a pile on my desk, and I decided that this was an issue for my deputy to resolve. Rupert had been working as a farm labourer in England for long enough; I needed him here, in Australia, but I couldn't afford to pay his fare.

Rupert's ambitions, upon boarding the aircraft at Heathrow, were uncomplicated – he simply wanted to walk to the North Pole. Royal Marine Commando training had moulded a quiet, thoughtful and methodical man with great inner strength, his motives perfectly fathomable. But he was confused about why the expedition's base had moved so far south. He had no idea how long he would be required to stay in the country, or if he could afford to do so, or indeed how on earth he was to begin sourcing Arctic equipment in Sydney. Four days after his arrival he gatecrashed a party, met Janet Hughes, a museum curator, fell instantly and desperately in love, and three weeks later was engaged to be married. Basing the expedition in Australia now made good sense to everyone.

It was Rupert's belief that one should choose one's Polar companions carefully; one may, after all, be forced to eat them. When Graeme Joy drove from Melbourne to Sydney to meet him, he little knew that he was to be the only applicant to endure a rigorous scrutiny. He emerged smiling to shake my hand. We were now three walking to the Pole. Meanwhile, on the other side of the world, a young black American had made up his mind to be the fourth.

✳

I met Darryl Roberts in his native city towards the end of 1987, a few months after delivering a speech to the Explorers' Club in New York. I had harangued the audience about the fact that the club's flag had flown on almost every piece of inhospitable terrain on earth, but it had never been unfurled in one of the world's toughest regions which lay just a few miles from where we were – in Harlem. The very next day I found myself crouched in a Red Cross truck with the club's president, travelling slowly through an urban nightmare of broken glass, rubble, and thwarted hopes. I was shocked by the wasteland around me. As I stared through the tiny windows of the truck I thought: instead of simply commemorating Peary's companion, Matthew Henson, why not include someone who could make a difference to the future here, in this place? Whoever he was, he could become a role model for these kids who could see nothing much beyond mugging, crack and lost hope.

On 21st October Darryl made his way to the Radio City Music Hall to meet Robert Swan, the Polar crusader. He knew the sort of role model kids needed, he told me. There were new drugs out there which were cheaper, which got you higher for shorter periods of time so that you needed more. Kids as young as nine or ten were selling crack. They needed someone to jump out of nowhere and scare them half to death. They didn't want lawyers, policemen and congressmen held up for their edification; they wanted someone to do something dangerous;

9 Darryl E. Roberts wanted to do something out of the ordinary
10 Matthew Henson – the unsung hero of Polar exploration

they wanted someone like them but a little insane to shine like a beacon of light.

Although Darryl was only 23 and had no expedition experience – and certainly no experience of the cold – I agreed he should be given a trial. He was to accompany the team on its first reconnaissance, funded by the Australian company Amatil, in April the following year, after which a team decision would be made as to his suitability. I didn't tell him so, but I was determined Darryl *would* be suitable.

The odds were against him from the start. Studies carried out by American military physicians have demonstrated an increased susceptibility to localised cold injury among certain groups. Blacks are thought to be three to six times more susceptible to frostbite than whites because they do not increase their heat production as efficiently, and begin shivering sooner at lower temperatures. This is believed to be the result of long residence in tropical climates, where heat dissipation is more essential than heat conservation. It was compounded in Darryl's case by a history of asthma. Yet I was taken with his engaging sense of humour and his commitment to helping New York's underprivileged children.

No such questions hung over our West German recruit. From the moment the bearded Arved Fuchs strode up to me in the foyer of the Congress Centrum in Hamburg and unfurled a huge navigational chart

11   Arved Fuchs – the West German explorer

of the Arctic ocean, I knew I had met a professional. Exploration was all that Arved did. He had huge, gentle eyes, a large generous smile, and an ease which had taken him to the tops of mountains, around Cape Horn in a kayak and across the frozen wastes by dogsled. Arved appeared strong, self-sufficient and, through years of exposure to the world's secret and wild places, committed to their preservation. It was not the Pole which mattered most to him, but Icewalk's mission of international endeavour – yet his admission to the team came about almost by accident.

Arved had planned to be nearing the end of an Antarctic expedition with Reinhold Messner early in 1989, but at almost the same moment as he heard that the journey was postponed for twelve months, he received a telephone call from a German magazine asking if he would be interested in contemplating the North Pole instead.

Over dinner in a crowded restaurant I asked Arved how far he would be prepared to take it under duress.

'If you developed severe frostbite, and pressing on meant the loss of several toes or fingers, would you go on, or go back?' I asked.

'Go back,' Arved said.

I paused, and thought of Roger Mear. Caution had been his watchword in the Antarctic.

'Correct answer,' I said. Safety was to be the expedition's first

12 Icewalk was Misha Malakhov's third major Arctic expedition
13 Hiro Onishi – one of Japan's leading mountaineers

priority. Leaning back in my chair, I swallowed my wine with a single gulp and toasted Arved's recruitment to the team with an empty glass. We stood and embraced across the table. We were now five walking to the Pole.

Japan was not so easy but I was determined to involve this important country. Eight months earlier, with the support of the Japanese Alpine Club I had managed to set in motion the machinery that now led to the recruiting of a first class mountaineer, Hiro Onishi, and after exercising more patience than I thought I had in me, I was able to secure the backing of *Yomiuri Shimbun*, one of the world's largest newspapers, and the commitment of their leading environmental correspondent Okajima-san. The real estate tycoon, Shingo Nomura, injected much needed cash into our fledgling operation and provided an office free of charge.

Meanwhile Rupert had become involved in a series of confidential communications with the Soviet Union. Letters were exchanged through a Soviet scientist visiting Sydney, and eventually a telephone call was put through to the renowned polar explorer, Dr Mikhail Malakhov. Excited by Icewalk's internationalism, Mikhail agreed to join us.

Still an eighth man was needed, and it struck me as both diplomatic

14 Angus (Kaanerk) Cockney, former Canadian cross-country ski-champion

and sensible for that person to be a Canadian. Not just any Canadian: I wanted an Inuit, an Eskimo. The Inuit people had watched generations of explorers make bid after desperate bid for the Pole. It was a pursuit regarded by most people of the North as crazy – 'There isn't much to see out there,' they said, 'and even less to eat.' Yet their predicament highlighted the Icewalk message so well: here were people being slowly poisoned by industrial effluent produced thousands of miles from their wild and remote home. Few had more reason than the Inuit to demonstrate their love for, and dependence upon, the Arctic's ferocious but vulnerable climate.

Angus Kaanerk Cockney, a former cross-country ski-champion, was selected to make up the expedition's full complement. We were all to meet together for the first time over Christmas during a brief training trip in Iqaluit (Frobisher Bay) on Baffin Island in Canada's North West Territories. The only question now – where was I to find the $3 million it would take to get us to the Pole?

✳

As my aircraft circled Grand Rapids Airport I stared at the beautiful autumnal landscape below. In these past few weeks I had been robbed of the expedition's last $2,000, I had met Senator Edward Kennedy, I had addressed the International Public Speakers Conference in Washington DC, and had spoken to Robert Redford after a brief visit to the actor's Institute for Resource Management. Now my quest for funds had taken me to the heart of middle America, a place I had never visited before.

The aircraft touched down and taxied towards the small terminal which was a microcosm of the local community – light, airy, neat and friendly. As I drove past the picturesque timber homes with their large unfenced gardens and clusters of trim trees, I subconsciously adjusted my tie and straightened the jacket of my suit. I had met the president of Amway Japan at a dinner party in Tokyo. Bill Hemmer, a keen outdoorsman, had liked our expedition and its aims, and here I was approaching Amway's headquarters in Ada, Michigan, fingers crossed.

I hoped it would be more than another day, another corporation. Even Peary had to be funded, and he often cited to potential sponsors the increased market penetration achieved by Lipton teas through Sir Thomas Lipton's involvement in international yacht racing. Yet once his funding had been secured, he did not concern himself overly with justifying the value of the expedition to his benefactors. In the early 1900s American companies would be well satisfied to have their name linked with the conquest of the North Pole.

Today companies require a firmer return on their investment, and an explorer's time is often equally divided between the boardroom and the great outdoors. I knew that I needed the help of someone experienced at high level public relations, and who better than Richard Down and his London-based company, Interaction Associates, which had done so much to ease the administrative nightmare of the South Pole expedition. Since that time the company had grown, and once again Richard lent both his personal and professional support – though this time at an international level. If a corporation was to express interest in Icewalk, I now had the necessary credentials to take negotiations that one step further.

Nothing, however, prepared me for the size of Amway's headquarters. The site was more than a mile long, bigger than the Pentagon. Employees were bussed from one area to another, and from this sprawling complex the company administered one and a half million sales representatives throughout the world.

The huge entrance foyer was dominated by statues and paintings of the Corporation's founders and owners, Rich De Vos and Jay Van Andel. The entire complex was the realisation of their dream, which had begun in a basement 30 years earlier. I embarked on a tour and was immediately struck by two things: one was the friendliness of the people, the other was the extent of the corporation's research facilities.

Amway was one of the first companies in the world to market biodegradable products, and had become one of the world's largest marketing networks, with a presence in more than forty countries. Yet the company's earliest days – of makeshift headquarters, improvisation, long hours and an energetic spirit of optimism – were clearly echoed in the Icewalk endeavour.

De Vos and Van Andel and their chief operating officer, Bill Nicholson, were open, enthusiastic and friendly. There was no need for Swan to battle his way up through an unyielding hierarchy here; instead I was welcomed as one of the family. I knew intuitively I had something to offer this company, and I knew they could make better use of the expedition and its objectives than almost any other organisation. What better way could there be than through this company's vast sales network to spread Icewalk's grassroots environmental message to those people who could make the most substantial difference – the world's families?

The company bade me farewell with a handful of airline tickets to keep the expedition moving northwards, and a promise from Dr Sam Rehnberg, the president of the sister company Nutrilite, to produce the world's most calorific chocolate bar for use on the Polar journey.

Three weeks later they summoned me back to Ada and presented me with a magnificent cheque.

At last Icewalk was going to the Pole.

2

THE END OF THE BEGINNING

I felt the cold rising through the fuselage of the aircraft as we flew north from Ottawa four months later. Far below the snow deepened, almost engulfing the dark shapes of the trees. Then, like a green wave running up a beach, the tide of firs quickly petered out and in one breath the landscape was transformed into something alien but strangely beautiful. Gentle bulges indicated hills; flat expanses, lakes. Ice castles rose trapped in frozen moats. We had entered the air-space of that most forbidding of natural environments, the Arctic.

The aircraft drifted gently earthward. It felt as though we were about to fall asleep on a huge crumpled sheet. The colours and textures of the frozen ocean changed with each dip of the wing. How many shades of pale are there?

Sir James Ross, one of the British polar explorers who put the 'loathsome shores' of the Arctic islands on the map during the last century, wrote of them as 'lands of uniformity, silence and death'. It was easy to see why. Barren and featureless, as if some divine architect had cemented the whole thing over, there are no points of reference for the eye, nowhere to stand and get a different perspective. The Arctic is vast and white and frightening, and it goes on for ever.

I wasn't sure that I was ready to face it. Indeed, I wasn't sure that Icewalk itself would be ready. Hundreds of miles to the south, in a house in the suburbs of the Canadian capital, the small but dedicated headquarters team was still grappling round the clock with a logistical nightmare of international proportions.

Eight expedition members in seven countries had precipitated a series of almost independent pre-expedition programmes. As a result, men and equipment that should have been in Ottawa lay scattered across every continent on earth, including Antarctica. To complicate

15 *Over page*: The frozen Arctic, alien but beautiful

matters even further, our principal sponsor was based in the United States while our finances were administered from England. The student expedition was being assembled from Lavinia Sidgwick's cottage in the Cotswolds, with assistance from the Duke of Edinburgh's Award Scheme in London. Lavinia was also trying to act as mission control for my non-stop globe-trotting activities, but no one person seemed to be in charge of the huge media campaign that was growing in leaps and bounds.

It grew worse. By the end of February the house was crammed to the eaves with the multinational base camp team, Australian journalists, English and German film crews, Japanese photographers and Soviet psychologists.

Lee Scott and student expedition leader Christopher Holloway had established headquarters in Ottawa, and Kirstie Hutchison, who had opened and closed Icewalk offices in Britain, Australia, Texas and Michigan, had not been far behind. Into this maelstrom of Customs documents and misplaced equipment strode Jim Hargreaves, recruited at the eleventh hour to bring some order to the operation. A seasoned adventurer in his own right, Jim had been the first man to canoe round Cape Horn. He had organised many major expeditions, but this promised to be his toughest assignment yet. Many essentials were either inadequate, damaged, or simply missing. Food had to be purchased and packaged. Medical programmes had to be salvaged, film crews equipped for Arctic conditions, hundreds of separate flights and charters co-ordinated.

In fact, as I stepped from the plane to be blasted by a wind that burned my lungs, I realised that the only thing I did know for sure was that the support team's task would be every bit as tough as ours while they battled to maintain the supply line from Ottawa north to Iqaluit, Resolute, Eureka, Cape Columbia and, finally, the Pole.

Iqaluit is a paradox. The houses are modern, heated, replete with satellite dishes; yet on most doorsteps rest the remains of last season's hunt. The streets echo to the high-pitched buzz of snowmobiles, but at night the only sound is the howling of sled dogs. The Inuit watch television and carve soap stone; they buy frozen fast foods and hunt seals and caribou.

In his beautiful study of the Inuit Hugh Brody asked: 'How can people use dog teams as well as snowmobiles? How can they live in both snow houses and prefabricated bungalows? How can they depend upon both the harpoon and the rifle? How can they be both Shamanistic and Christian? How can they exist, at one and the same

16 Iqaluit – our home for almost a month

time, in the past and the present?'

Many could not. This place had one of the highest adolescent suicide rates in the country. What would the local kids make of Icewalk's 22 student expedition members? I was saddened by the knowledge that, because I would be out on the ice at the time, I would be unable to share what was really most important to me.

We drove to our apartment in White Row Housing and managed to turn another respectable dwelling into a shambles within hours of arrival. The disorganisation I had already sensed in Ottawa was more apparent here. Misha Malakhov said of the team, 'The men are good, but lack polar experience. They not know what they do. They should learn how to follow advice.'

As Misha pointed out, on the ice a small personal problem can become a big team problem. I realised I was one of the worst culprits; this was the first time I had given proper thought to the expedition since conjuring the whole thing up in Antarctica. Getting the show on the road in the first place had taken all my time and attention.

Despite everything, I am forced to admit to being something of a reluctant explorer. I abhor the concept of training. I loathe the cold,

hate camping, have rarely ventured into an outdoor store, don't particularly enjoy fiddling with stoves or adjusting ski-bindings, and would do anything to avoid sitting beside a guttering flame to dry my thermals. Sheer bloody-mindedness got me to the South Pole, and I hoped it would stand me in good stead again. I do not consider myself a member of the small and highly competitive clique of the world's elite explorers and mountaineers. In many ways I have forced myself into a profession which ill-suits me. Yet, here I was with a team to shepherd – and that's where I come into my own.

While the team prepared for its first short training session out on the sea ice, a difficult decision was looming. With my lack of practical skills I had no intention of taking the lead out on the ice. This position had been Rupert's from the outset. Rupert was my deputy, and had spent two years equipping the expedition. Now, after travelling thousands of miles to Iqaluit, he was about to board another aircraft and return to Australia for the birth of his first child.

Because of Misha's experience it seemed natural for him to assume a position of authority in Rupert's absence.

'I am unhappy with preparations,' he said to me one evening. 'It seems to me we have, er, too many discussions and not have enough time. We must take, ah . . . you would call it . . . hard line. I do not want to be . . .' He furrowed his brow.

'Dictatorial?' I offered.

'Yes, dictatorial. You should tell team – from this moment we have few discussions. We use my experience. It will be difficult for me and for them, but it will be our best chance. If you do not do this I cannot be sure our travel will be successful.'

The team did not readily accept this decision; Misha had not been involved with Icewalk for as long as many of the others. While the discussions continued, increasingly he and I found ourselves working together, with Misha making most of the practical decisions, then referring them through me to the team.

Rupert seemed philosophical about the powerplay taking place. Recent changes had altered the entire fabric of the expedition, and I knew he would have liked it to have been different.

'What we have done is to organise an expedition from scratch in six weeks. Unfortunately, it has been organised the wrong way round. We've involved countries and then tried to find expedition members;

17 Preparing rations in Iqaluit
18 Rupert tests an amphibious sledge

we should have located expedition members first. That way you get a consensus, not necessarily a compromise.'

Graeme was also concerned. 'Our leadership isn't as strong as it should be,' he said. 'The whole exercise has been allowed to run too much on individual lines. Robert is not a field leader. Rupert's absence will be disruptive. Misha is too dogmatic, and so am I. I think it is Robert's responsibility to re-instate Rupert. Until this happens we are stuck with a sort of gipsy's caravan that might make it to the Pole, but is going to have a lot of problems along the way.'

The leadership issue was left unresolved, and I hoped things would eventually assume a natural order. Fortunately the constant to-ing and fro-ing did not erode team spirit. Most discussions were disrupted by wild laughter; the language and cultural barriers were a source of amusement rather than irritation.

Darryl spent long hours helping Hiro with his English, translating James Brown lyrics into Japanese. Most equipment meetings dragged on into the evening as Misha referred constantly to his English dictionary, holding up his hand like a traffic warden as people called him to hurry up. One evening I found him alone in a tent, sitting cross-legged and staring intently at three different types of stove, all burning furiously. He was determined the Soviet stove be chosen, despite its propensity to explode.

19 The Soviet tent system used skis to save weight

Eventually we pressed out on to the ice for a three-day reconnoitre. We struggled across the bay which abuts Iqaluit. My sledge was a disaster. We pitched camp and tested the Soviet tent for the first time, the same version as was used on the Polar Bridge expedition. Our skis formed the tent frame – an excellent weight-saving device.

That first morning we had two rather alarming incidents. Misha insisted on mixing the pemmican with the muesli and then burnt the lot to the bottom of the pot. It was without doubt the worst food I had ever tasted. Hiro asked for more.

The second was far more serious. The Soviet stove just went crazy. Within seconds the tent was on fire. Misha dived into action, kicked a hole in one of the tent's panels, and threw the stove outside. It landed on Arved's feet as he stood admiring the view.

Before striking camp, we had spotted a smudge on the horizon moving swiftly in our direction. It was Brent Boddy, one of the north's leading dog-handlers, and his team. The dogs pounded towards us, a cloud of snow dust engulfing them, pink tongues flashing, whip cracking. Brent in caribou skins issued sharp commands in Inuktitut. The dogs overran the film crew, who were shadowing us, knocking the cameraman to the ground. Brent was accompanied by a small convoy of locals on snowmobiles ferrying journalists and photographers. I gazed at the local men reclining on their machines like Arctic cowboys. At $100 per machine per day, I calculated what the expedition was costing per minute, and I could have done with a strong drink.

During the afternoon we managed to escape from the paparazzi and forged out across the flat ice towards the setting sun. It wasn't too cold; in fact it was quite warm and very beautiful. I asked Misha if he was happy. He didn't answer. I asked him again, several times.

'I am happy,' he said reluctantly, 'but the journey to Pole will be very difficult. I know team members are clever, but I am concerned they do not trust – ah – my recommendations. It is difficult to appreciate what will be like in Cape Columbia when Iqaluit is so comfortable.'

The team were enjoying the day, the sun shone and the air was as crisp as new paper. During our lunch break Hiro grabbed a ski pole and drew a large circle in the snow. He invited Darryl into the circle and then attempted, with grins and gestures, to explain the rudiments of Sumo wrestling. They each picked up a handful of snow from within the ring and threw it out; they bent hands on knees and eyed each other warily. Then Hiro, who must weigh all of 120 lbs, lifted the 200 lb Darryl clean out of the ring.

We pitched camp that evening in the middle of nowhere. I slept

badly. The winds howled across the frozen sea, shaking the tent toothless. I awoke, suddenly convinced we were about to lose the thing. Everyone else was asleep. I clambered outside and the full force of the gale struck me. It was around minus 40 degrees celsius, but the wind chill factor must have dropped the temperature closer to minus 70. I moved slowly around the tent, shovelling snow against its base. Suddenly I saw the most astonishing sight. Arved's head was poking out from beneath the tent. He was snoring loudly, oblivious to the cold fury of the near gale force winds. I poked him back into the tent. Fortunately he suffered only minor frostbite to his nose.

The film crew arrived on skidoos to capture us decamping the next morning. We were impressed by their persistence. At minus 80 (with windchill) it was as cold as we were likely to encounter on the journey itself, and colder than it had ever been in Antarctica.

We tackled some pressure ridges. Arved found the going difficult with his larger sledge; he and I despised backpacks. I had thought it best to travel with a system with which we felt most comfortable. Misha, however, argued that the larger sledges would be a hindrance not only to ourselves but also the group. Gus and Graeme adapted to the pressure ridges very quickly; they were both natural sportsmen. Hiro found them more difficult.

We pitched camp as it grew dark. Everyone was weary and moved about slowly. It had been a long, desperately cold day. Darryl sat in a cold tent without boots and without socks. Misha became furious with Gus for losing the saucepan lid, a minor occurrence but without it the water took forever to boil.

Graeme managed a successful radio transmission, but as we joked later, if all else failed we could simply have shouted. We were only a mile from town. It was odd to be able to see the soft lights of Iqaluit on the horizon and hear the low drone of aircraft as they landed, and yet know that one mistake even this close to civilization and toes or fingers could be lost.

✳

The following evening, almost eight hours after our return to Iqaluit, Darryl discovered he had frostbite to his toes. He sat propped against the wall in his crowded bedroom. Hiro lay on the floor massacring the

20 *Previous page*: Training near Iqaluit

21 After many test runs all but Robert and Arved opted for a combination of
    backpack and small sledge

22 The distant lights of Iqaluit

23 Robert inspects Darryl's frostbitten toes

English language. Misha was down on all fours, prodding Darryl's foot with a sharp pencil.

'Sharp, sharp, pressure, pressure, sharp,' Darryl exclaimed, indicating the areas where numbness had taken hold. Misha scowled. The first and second toes of the left foot were blue; the others were also scorched but not as badly. There was little feeling in the injured areas. Liquid could be seen under the skin; blisters would soon follow. Misha knew it was serious.

'Tell me man, I want to know what is going on,' Darryl muttered, shifting uncomfortably.

'I will explain,' Misha said softly, then didn't.

Hiro and I joked throughout this macabre procedure. We could see the look of fear in Darryl's eyes. Misha explained the symptoms to me in whispered tones, then moved on to Hiro's feet, which were blistered, and then Arved's frostbitten nose.

Two hours later Misha knocked at the door of my room to give me the prognosis on Darryl. 'I do not think he will be going,' he said flatly.

3

STRANGERS IN A STRANGE LAND

In deep cold, steel shatters like porcelain when dropped on a hard surface. Flesh is scorched. The cold drives blunt needles through your bones. It kills.

Survival is down to self-discipline and training, little tricks like not blowing on your hands to warm them because the vapour of your breath freezes instantly, forming ice on the eyebrows and in the nose. You must never drop your guard. The cold waits until your back is turned, then it attacks. Darryl had turned his back. He had sat in the tent with nothing on his feet.

Exposure for as little as one or two minutes is enough to induce frostbite: hard, cold patches of skin insensitive to touch. If the condition is allowed to take hold, part of the body shuts down, sacrificing an extremity – most commonly a toe or a finger – rather than risking the death of the whole body. To prevent the body core temperature falling below the danger level the blood refuses to go into the cold area. Tissues and nerves freeze up and are deprived of nutrition and oxygen. Ultimately the affected part simply falls off. Even in its mildest form frostbite is dangerous.

Within twenty-four hours Darryl's toes had blistered and he was in excruciating pain, barely able to hobble from his bedroom to the kitchen at the end of the apartment's short corridor. A strange sort of hardness settled over the team. There had been smiles and handshakes all round when Darryl had first met the team in Resolute, but behind this general air of congeniality Graeme and Rupert harboured fears that the inexperienced young American would not prove an able candidate. Rupert had spent the better part of his career in the Antarctic and Arctic regions, and Graeme, an accomplished canoeist, had survived a treacherous traverse of Greenland's East Coast. In training, Darryl had already contracted mild frostbite in temperatures of minus 30 degrees celsius. A local doctor who specialised in cold

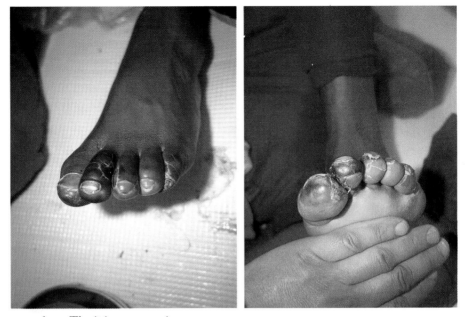

24 and 25 The injury was serious

weather disabilities diagnosed Raynaud's phenomenon, a condition where muscles surrounding the arteries to the hands and feet constrict in cold conditions, inhibiting the flow of blood. The doctor prescribed a medication to thin the blood and advised Darryl to increase his percentage of body fat prior to the expedition.

Rupert was concerned that my selection of Darryl had been purely emotional, with no real thought given to his practical experience or physical suitability. If Darryl died out there on the ice . . .

A weakened team member slowed not only himself but the whole team; he jeopardised not only his own chances of victory – or even survival – but everyone else's as well. I was aware that the others felt this as strongly as I did.

I sat in my room trying to push the problem to the back of my mind as I sewed and made minor adjustments to my kit. Serious frostbite was a problem I had hoped none of us would have to face. In the warmth and calm of our Iqaluit apartment the solution was simple. I knew it; Misha knew it; Darryl knew it. Darryl need not begin the final leg of his journey, risk the loss of toes, nor face the prospect of evacuation.

Misha did not discuss the problem with anyone but me and clearly wished to withhold his judgment until as late as possible. He took Darryl to the local hospital for a second opinion. The news was not encouraging.

Darryl had made a mistake. I felt sorry for him, and concerned, though I was determined that this mistake would not jeopardise his chances. Our first priority was for eight men to arrive at the Pole together and in safety. The fact that we might not didn't bear thinking about.

After returning from hospital Darryl hobbled down the corridor to my room and edged his body awkwardly through the door.

'How was it?' I asked without looking up.

'Awful, man,' he said. 'They have to take two toes . . .'

I paused, my needle in mid-stitch, and slowly raised my eyes to his. He stood grinning back at me.

'How?' I asked ghoulishly.

'With a hot butter knife.' His normally infectious laugh echoed hollow that day.

We both fell silent.

Darryl sighed and shifted his injured foot. 'Actually, Robert, the hospital doesn't know what to make of it. They suspect that it's nasty. They have never seen a black with frostbite to the toes and don't know what colour they should be. When my skin is damaged it gets darker, so I'm hoping it looks worse than it actually is. They told me to stay off my feet for the next few days, and Misha will monitor my progress.'

I gritted my teeth. Only days remained before we departed for the Pole. He had come this far; how could he now just sit and wait and see?

'Let's face it, if this doesn't clear up, you won't be walking anywhere, except to hospital,' I said. 'But if it does, you're fit and healthy – your chances are good. You must look after your feet and not get angry, because if you get angry you'll get depressed, and then you'll give in. You can't just wait and see.'

I went back to sewing while I delivered the lecture.

'You must get your personal gear sorted out. I don't want to hear you complain about your ski-bindings coming undone all the time. Fix them. Don't lie on your bed. Sit on a hard surface; keep your feet comfortable, but sit on a hard surface. If you remain this disorganised you will not be able to go. You know, Darryl, you sat in that tent the other night with your boots and socks off. Why? Because you didn't have any spare socks to put on. You've got to get the system going. You know me; I'm the laziest person in the whole world. I refuse to sew unless I have to. I'm not doing this for any other reason than I don't want to get frostbite – I don't want to die.'

Darryl returned to his lair and worked alone quietly. During the following days the team became united in their support for him. Many realised that it could just as easily have been them. We all realised that it was too late to turn back now. Too late for any of us.

✳

The days passed quickly as people repaired sledges, waxed skis, sliced salami, weighed butter and convened meeting after meeting. Nothing ever seemed to be resolved. Rupert returned from Australia exhausted but elated: he was now the father of a baby girl. He attempted to regain the driving seat, but if any one real leader was emerging it was Misha, though he was far from gaining the team's compliance.

The discussions continued. What fur for the jacket hoods, wolf or dog? Misha said fox fur was too short. Which stoves? The Soviet ones were best, said Misha. Where were the spare socks? Would Graeme's vapour barrier system for the sleeping bags prove effective? Who was to weigh the food rations? Could longer skis be obtained this late? Misha refused to set off without longer skis. Would we sleep in one tent or two? Misha argued we could do without the seven kilogram weight of the second tent. Days and nights passed.

Apartment life remained chaotic. I often retreated with my sleeping bag and slept outside. Minus 35 degrees celsius, but at least I was alone, could smoke a cigarette and stare at the Northern skies, allowing my thoughts to be drawn into the infinity of the Aurora Borealis. Listening to the distant, groaning ocean I could hear a chorus of lost voices trapped beneath the ice but could only guess at what they were saying. I stared at our lighted windows and watched the shadowy figures of my friends moving from room to room.

Photographers, Japanese journalists and film crews came and went; there were early morning satellite television interviews; film messages to record for the student expedition; the giving of blood to the good doctor at the local hospital; contracts and business to be dealt with over the telephone; afternoon talks to local school children; and product photographic shoots for sponsors. I wondered if I would ever finish repairing my old sledge.

Darryl hobbled from the apartment for the sponsor shoot, crawling up and sliding down the pressure ridges holding a chocolate bar aloft and grinning widely for the cameras. Misha had a boxful of small flags and banners from his sponsors and supporters in the Soviet Union. He was a well known figure in Soviet exploration circles and a well connected and tireless entrepreneur. He was also one of the world's leading experts on the treatment of frostbite in the field and a North

26 Darryl, Gus and Graeme pose for the expedition's sponsors

Pole veteran, having completed the arduous Polar Bridge Expedition the previous year (a gruelling journey from the Soviet side of the Arctic Ocean, across the Pole to Canada's northern shores). He had obtained funding for Icewalk from private individuals and companies, a practice almost unheard of in the Soviet Union. The Rjazan Machine Tool Manufacturing Amalgamation was Misha's principal sponsor.

∗

The morning skies were suffused with a deceptively warm glow. The ice swirled alabaster and azure. Sometimes I stood on the unprotected plains behind the township to gaze out at the ocean which pushed its claws into the hills. Nothing moved in the early hours but for five or six sinister shadows which rippled across the bay. Ravens, giant black ravens – the only bird to winter this far north. Uttering their guttural cries, the birds scavenged the town's streets.

In 1860 McLintock spoke in his Polar diaries of the raven who 'alone scorns to change either his colour or his clime.' McLintock records seeing ravens in the depths of a winter's darkness illuminated briefly by starlight. Occasionally his party shot a bird to find it missing some of its toe joints – the result of frostbite.

All over the Arctic regions they have been found: the same bird

27 Arved, Hiro, Gus, Graeme, Robert, Misha, Darryl, Rupert

which still hovers over the sweltering plains of Jericho, and lodges in the rocky hill-side which overhangs the brook Cherith; the same wonderful bird which the early Vikings, we are told, took with them upon their voyages, somewhat in the double capacity of mariner's compass and chief pilot – their extraordinary powers of sight and smell enabling them to discover land at incredible distances.

So here we were, the ravens and I, strangers in a strange land. Whether our team could hope to be as adaptable and resourceful as they were was yet to be determined.

✳

The base camp crew worked round the clock weighing and preparing food, building bunks for the Polar haven, testing the stoves and tracking down the items of equipment that were still in transit from Ottawa and places further afield. Stephen Williams began battling with what he knew already was inadequate radio equipment; Jeremy Morris plugged in his Apple Macintosh and tried to locate Toulouse, where the Argos Satellite tracking service was based. The Argos retrospective position locating system operated off two or more satellites which received the signals transmitted by our beacons in the evening. Our position was then beamed into the system's mainframe computer in Toulouse in France, and was then retrieved by Jeremy in Resolute using an Apple modem link. We could also transmit very basic coded messages to Jeremy via Toulouse in the event of an extended radio blackout. This code ranged from 'Please send more sleeping bags' to 'Please send the Royal Canadian Mounted Police search and rescue unit'.

And all the while local women made the final adjustments to our clothing, chewing our seal skin boots into shape.

As the day of departure for Cape Columbia drew near, our meetings became more argumentative and tense. Rupert struggled to smooth out as many difficulties as possible. For some days Misha had been arguing for a new, longer type of ski (210 centimetres rather than 190) with a middle gutter which he believed made them more stable. On countless occasions I, along with Rupert and Graeme, had assured him that

28 The team adopted many Inuit survival techniques including sealskin kamiks

29 Radio operator, Stephen Williams, arrived in Iqaluit to be confronted with a host of technical problems

Headquarters was doing its best to locate such a ski, but to no avail.

As we sat on the floor of our crowded apartment, checking food lists and fiddling with stoves and sextants, Misha doggedly raised the issue again. The most infuriating thing about Misha was that he was almost always right. That afternoon I found myself shouting – for the first time – at the startled doctor.

'Do get it into your brain once and for all that these skis you want will not be available for the first eight days of the journey.'

The others stared in silence. They had not seen us argue before. Misha remained calm.

'Robert, Robert, I am very boring for you, but I, ah, think of others. They will have big trouble without correct skis.'

At that moment the telephone rang. The skis had been found.

'Yippee,' I said sarcastically.

Misha stared at me blankly. 'You see! You emotion, I persistent.'

'And lucky,' I replied curtly.

'But you angry with me. Why?'

'It's better than sulking.'

Misha stared at me, then stood to leave.

'Yes, go and get your dictionary,' I called after him as he left the room. 'S-U-L-K-I-N-G.'

The others began talking quietly to fill the embarrassing silence. I marched back to my room. Misha's determination sometimes drove us to the edge. But we had to remember that he was not simply being argumentative; he knew where we were going and what was needed to stay alive. I was sorry we had argued.

Differences of opinion persisted nevertheless. How much fuel would be required for each day of rest? Misha wanted 60 litres, almost ten times as much as Rupert had made provision for. Misha argued it would be needed to dry clothes and keep the tent warm for the arduous medical and scientific programmes. I walked into the middle of this debate and proclaimed to Graeme and Rupert that we must go for full excess on the day of rest.

'Sixty litres of fuel per person per day,' I announced. 'A roaring bonfire.'

'We're talking greenhouse effect,' Rupert put in.

Misha stared at all three of us without smiling and then returned impatiently to his lists of calculations.

Sledges were another bone of contention. Arved's and my monsters were certainly out of favour. So was Rupert's amphibious prototype, which he hoped would be adopted later in the journey when we faced the menace of open water. North Pole expeditions which have attempted to use larger sledges have on the whole been unsuccessful, Misha argued. They had only achieved their goal when they did not haul more than 40 kilograms at any one time.

'We will carry 50 or 60 kilograms. To add 16 kilogram weight of sledge is foolish,' Misha said.

Misha's words jolted me. I thought of a passage I had read recently in Berton's *The Arctic Grail*: 'Scott and his men, dragging their heavy sledges on foot, died of hunger and exhaustion. Roald Amundsen, the Norwegian, beat them to the Pole, ate his dogs and lived. Strangely, to the English there was something noble, something romantic, about strong young men marching in harness through the Arctic wastes, enduring incredible hardships with a smile on their lips and a song in their hearts. They were like the knights of old, breaking new paths, facing unknown perils in their search for the Grail.'

Berton's tone was too harsh. Scott had not entered into a race, his sledges when found were laden with geological specimens. In the Arctic the English were not made foolish by their blind search for the grail; if anything it was their inability to adapt to the place they found themselves in, their refusal to adopt the survival and travelling methods of the local Inuit which impeded their progress. The passage of time has made them appear unwisely proud.

My preference for the sledge was neither romantic nor stubborn. It was just that I loathed the pack – it hurt my back, which had been considerably weakened during the South Pole journey. I could not be bothered explaining this to Misha, whose sentiments so loudly echoed Berton's.

I began withdrawing once again, deciding that Rupert, Graeme and Misha could sort things out between themselves. Instead I concentrated on contracts. Misha neither approved nor understood my preoccupation. 'Now is not time to raise money,' he warned sternly. 'Principal position, ah, to be inside expedition – not outside.'

It was all very well for him – he wasn't paying for the thing.

I tried to be inside. I had lived in a complete and utter whirl for three years and now here I was on the eve of our departure for Cape Columbia. Three years ago I had had the time and a deep rooted obsession with Scott and Antarctic exploration to sustain me. If they could do it, I could do it: it was that simple. The history, the romance, the pathos – these were the things I had loved about the South.

This was a very different affair, more complicated and with higher stakes. Yet it was not without passion. I wanted to cry when earlier that

30   The eve of departure for Cape Columbia, the northern tip of Ellesmere Island

day poor little Hiro heard word he had lost his friend to a mountain. I could see it in his eyes and how tightly he pushed the telephone against his ear. I could feel his sadness, and we shared it silently. There was a passion amongst this strange group. We were an international team but we *were* a team. If Hiro could make it, so could I; if Misha could, of course I could. We were in this together.

The final countdown. Rupert pinned the latest long term weather forecast to the wall. The Arctic winter had been milder than average, but a recent cold spell had brought a return to seasonal norms, it said. Already a number of large leads could be seen in satellite photographs. Disturbingly, they were tending north west to south east, whereas in previous years they had inclined northerly. This shift in trend did not bode altogether well. Neither did it hint at the desperate drama about to unfold.

4

THE STING OF THE HARNESS

'As soon as he saw the Big Boots, Pooh knew that an Adventure was going to happen . . .'

And for the first time it felt like an adventure. The 'big boots', along with a mountain of equipment – tents, skis, sledges, food, camera gear, medical kits, sleeping bags and cumbersome polar clothing – were crammed into the gullet of the old Boeing 748. The nets were removed from the aircraft's dark interior and equipment was heaved into every last remote recess. A thick fog swirled from out of the blackness and across the tarmac to surround us. The night was filled with the excited yells and laughs of the men, the sound of vehicles coughing in the cold, and the loud crunching of boxes and crates as they were dragged across the icy apron.

Our final twenty-four hours in Iqaluit had been charged with drama as we raced to complete our final tasks. Anxious for the safe return of his first samples of blood and urine to Ottawa General Hospital, Misha persuaded a Bradley's stewardess to hand-carry them on the next flight south. Johnny, a local Inuit Jack-of-all-trades, and Jens Steenberg, a carpenter, helped Arved and me to make the final alterations to our large, controversial sledges. Rupert, charging about in a last minute panic, exhibited the first signs of excitement. This cheered me tremendously; he had worked harder than anyone to get us this far. Gus was obviously nervous, his natural nonchalance now stretched very thin. Arved was as calm as ever. He was the only one to share my sense of the absurdity of what we were doing.

Misha fired off telexes of farewell to the Soviet Union; everyone except Arved had their hair cut. The school teacher in Graeme came into his own as he organised the ferrying of equipment.

I was worried about Hiro. He scurried about like a field mouse hauling loads twice his size. I was worried because I never quite knew what he was thinking; if he was concerned or afraid. We had paused to

55

talk a few evenings earlier as he crouched alone in a tent testing the expedition's large assortment of stoves.

'Hiro,' I asked him, 'do you think this walk will be difficult?'

'Walking is not difficult,' he replied. 'Walking is easy. Camping will be difficult. Sleeping will be difficult. Keeping dry will be difficult. I do not like the cold.'

He laughed, but I learned later, when we flew from Eureka to Cape Columbia, that his greatest concern was also mine.

'Must arrive as team,' he said. 'Darryl endure much. When sleeping, Darryl in centre. Check feet every day; it will be difficult.'

Neither of us was to know on that evening of 16th March just how difficult as we prepared to begin the final chapter. Despite the uncertainty clouding his future, Darryl had fought on and stood ready to join the team. Nothing more had been said about his condition in recent days. Misha had diligently dressed the wound and photographed its progress. A final decision was to be made in Cape Columbia but there were those who were unhappy with even the remote prospect of him setting out. If frostbite was to prove such a predator in temperatures of only minus 35 degrees celsius, what sort of brute would it become when the thermometer plunged to the low fifties?

At 8.30 p.m. the old 748 lumbered into the sky, gorged to the bulkheads with men and equipment. We banked lazily over tiny Iqaluit and the last fading lights of civilization. I put my hand on Teddy in my pocket. The rather tattered and tired animal had been to the South Pole, and hoped to become the first bear in history to see both. We all carried our good luck charms, small links with the world we were about to leave behind.

We sat hunched in our seats. There was barely room to move. For the most part we drifted silently into our own thoughts, staring at the darkness beyond our small windows. The film crew clattered up and down the aisle. Our departure had been a lonely one; I think we all felt a little empty inside.

We landed briefly in the bleak settlement of Resolute to refuel, and trooped across to the Bradley First Air office to see how Jeremy Morris was coping. He lived in a cluttered storeroom, its front door decorated with caribou horns and Christmas lights. He had cleared a space on a grimy wooden bench for the Apple Macintosh and filled the storeroom with provisions for the expedition's first resupply flight. His radio hissed erratically; we were still unsure how effectively the Cape Columbia/Resolute link would work. The kind of calendar garage mechanics covet decorated the wall. Jeremy loped about, his army

31 Jeremy Morris manned the radio in Resolute

fatigue pants drooping to his knees, readily sliding into the unhurried pace of life of this far northern settlement. With perpetual daylight, perpetual darkness and unpredictable weather the chief boundaries of existence, time was irrelevant.

We ate sandwiches and drank two cartons of Sir Ranulph Fiennes' beer (he had already left for the Pole) before heading north again. As we chugged back into the air I gazed down on that inhospitable settlement where polar bears can roam the streets during the winter darkness and people spend months indoors waiting for the sun to appear. I thought of Jeremy shuffling from storeroom to storeroom, his hair standing on end, and I smiled to myself. Several thousand feet below us a young Sydney law student stood in a dirty crowded back room of one of the world's remotest airline offices preparing to monitor the satellite tracking of eight men as they walked across a frozen piece of water. It was something he had not done before.

At 5 a.m. on the morning of Friday, 17th March, we landed with a loud thud in Eureka, the Canadian Government's high Arctic weather station. The aircraft doors slid open and the chilling Polar air rushed in thick and pungent as smoke. We were close now. The small cocooned community of Eureka welcomed us warmly. As the sun climbed higher into the sky we unloaded our mass of equipment in preparation for its transfer to two Twin Otters and onward shuttle to the Cape Columbia

32 Landing in Eureka, on the way to Cape Columbia

advance base. A pack of long-legged wolves crept on to the runway scavenging among our supplies. The wild north had come down to meet us.

At 80 degrees north the cold had a greater expanse to its girth. Minus 45 degrees celsius; just its slow pronunciation formed ice in one's mouth. We trekked along the snow-covered tarmac past Eureka's gaggle of miniature airport buildings which were almost completely buried in deep snow. Someone had painted an elaborate McDonalds frontage to one of the tiny makeshift huts. We drove the short distance to the weather station, which stood on the shores of a frozen fjord. The bay was ringed by gentle white mountains, and out of the fjord, with the stealth and mystery of the Loch Ness monster, rose the occasional iceberg.

The town square's civic monuments consisted of two musk oxen skulls, whale bones and a pink plastic flamingo. We threw open the huge 12-inch thick door to the weather station and hurried in, locking it behind us. Eureka's population of six were tremendously hospitable. The men tucked in as if they would never eat again and spent the day relishing a number of lasts – last meal at a table, last shower (I declined; I had not showered for three weeks in an effort to build up natural body oils as a further insulation against the cold), last glimpse of a television screen, last beer, last chair, last bed.

Before dusk we ski'd across the fjord to visit 'Churchberg', a towering, mint-blue monolith soaring more than 30 metres in the air. It was a dazzling thing. The ice shifted and sighed as black waters moved deep beneath it. A sharp sound like a gunshot echoed from within the giant as it tried to rock and heave itself free of its frozen mooring. As I trailed along the white shoreline I thought of the explorers of old trapped for entire winters in darkness in fjords like this, their timber ships struggling against the ice. Suffering from scurvy, shivering in stalactite-filled cabins, they whiled away the long dark days fighting the pull of depression and madness. The Polar Inuit called the winter blues *perlerorneq* – 'the weight of life'.

For me, the weight of the expedition melted away. Tomorrow life would be simple; I would have only two preoccupations – to stay alive and to nail the Pole.

✻

The team were nowhere to be seen. I asked Misha where everyone had gone. 'Sex film,' he replied curtly. He was clearly angry. I was astonished. No one had told me about it.

'Maybe forget they go to Pole in two days,' he said.

'Or maybe they've remembered,' I replied.

None of the equipment had been weighed or distributed. Misha worked silently through the night weighing everyone's gear and allocating it. The others could not tear themselves away from the world we were about to leave.

The following morning we began the final leg of our journey to Canada's northernmost point. Arved, Hiro, Misha and I were to fly in the first Twin Otter and the others were to follow later. The little aircraft whirred to life and we bounced and skidded along Eureka's bleak runway. We banked over the fjord and headed north. Flying low, we swooped over mountain ridges layered like dominoes and narrow, deathly-still fjords. It was a landscape beyond time. No trees; no visible life; absolute stillness.

Huge, motionless glaciers, like white hot lava, jutted into frozen seas where they shattered into hundreds of icebergs. Great shards of ice filled the estuaries. Glaciers brimmed to the very top of mountain valleys and then seemed to drain away forever.

Squashed into the aircraft's noisy cabin, we smiled at each other. The bone-crunching rattle discouraged conversation, so we drifted back into the hoods of our jackets and gazed at the alien world below. It was 18th March and I knew Misha was worried. We were departing

almost two weeks behind schedule. The team had simply not been ready to leave earlier.

Other expeditions were at least one week out – the Japanese Mako Expedition on snowmobiles; Pam Flowers making a solo attempt with a dog team. Sir Ranulph Fiennes and Dr Mike Stroud, who spent a year in the Antarctic with the Footsteps of Scott Expedition, had set out and returned already. Fiennes was making a third attempt at an unsupported assault on the Pole but deep snow had made it impossible for him to continue after only three days. I was sure he and Micky would make one last effort before abandoning the season. On the other side of the Arctic Ocean a Soviet team was also mounting an unsupported expedition but we knew little of their progress.

We had still to fix an exact time of departure, assuming it would be the day after tomorrow. Somewhere below us and to the north these people were already on their way. We had many miles to make up, but I tried not to think about that now; it was enough just to begin.

Two-and-a-half hours after leaving Eureka we started our descent into Cape Columbia. A blizzard engulfed the peninsula and visibility was almost nil. Our aircraft bounced and skidded to an abrupt halt along this last frozen promontory of land and we grimaced ruefully at each other. This was my first glimpse of the Arctic Ocean and my first

33 Ellesmere's frowning mountains
34 Five Twin Otter flights were required to transfer the team and its equipment to Cape Columbia

35 The Polar Haven at advance base

taste of the reward for three years' work. Misha had been here before. In May 1988 Rupert, Darryl and Graeme had also visited this area as part of the expedition's Amatil reconnaissance. Strangely I felt nothing; no excitement; no fear. Very suddenly it had begun.

We leapt from the comparative warmth of the aircraft and scurried off into the cold. The Base Camp team, led by Crispin Day, just back from two years in Antarctica, had arrived a day earlier to erect the large domed Polar Haven. This was to be home to ex-British Antarctic Survey radio operator Stephen Williams, Australian builder Dean Sassella, Londoner and old 'Footsteps' hand Keith Stanwyck, and Japanese law student Yoshi Ishikawa.

Stephen was struggling to establish radio communications during a time when all seemed set against him. This season scientists had predicted some of the worst ionospheric disturbances in decades. This solar flare activity played havoc with communications across Northern Canada but posed far more critical problems for our expedition. For this was not going to be the life or death dash to the South Pole, where we travelled without radios, knowing we had no hope of rescue if

36 The advance base camp team had arrived several days earlier

something went wrong. This time radios were to be our life source. Stephen was deeply concerned.

Hiro and I spent the day staggering about in the blizzard, helping Stephen to rig up wiring and secure the Polar Haven. The haven was divided into three small rooms; Dean's ready-built wooden bunks were in place and the front room was stacked high with provisions. The moist air was heavy with the stench of kerosene heaters and the fox den closeness of men living and working in small plastic rooms. As darkness gathered and there was still no sign of the remainder of the team we realised the poor weather must have grounded their flight.

We settled in for the evening. Supper was a raucous affair.

I wrote letters and cards of farewell and thought of home. We had received messages of goodwill and good luck from President Bush, Prime Ministers Thatcher, Mulroney, Hawke, Gandhi and Ryzhkov of the USSR; from Prince Charles; from Japan's Minister of the Environment; from the United Nations; from Will Steger and other Polar travellers; from sponsors, supporters, friends and family. Those farewells seemed to have been bid a lifetime ago.

Sunday, 19th March, dawned a little clearer. It was around minus 35 degrees celsius; perhaps a little too warm. Ellesmere's frowning mountains could be seen clearly to the south; and north – north lay the Pole.

The frozen ocean spread forever, and the ice, at the mercy of the northern tides, relentlessly ploughed back towards shore piling and crumpling up on itself. It looked like a great bombed city; the white rubble spread as far as the eye could see. The immensity and power of the place surged through me. We would not be skiing out gently on to a misty Antarctic plain; here someone had contrived a devilish obstacle course. I did not gaze at the ocean for long.

Misha cast a professional eye over the horizon and predicted difficult travel exacerbated by reports of soft snow, the same snow which had defeated Fiennes and his large sledge. We ventured out briefly on to the pack to the east of Cape Columbia and took stock of what lay ahead.

Stephen worked all day to establish radio contact with Resolute but to no avail. He eventually located Fiennes' base camp on Ward Hunt Island and received confirmation that Fiennes had returned, but we could not speak to our people. In the early afternoon the remainder of the team arrived, Darryl among them. It was strange how much we had missed them for that one evening, and I realised what a peculiar but close-knit group we had become through these long weeks of discussion, argument, rancour and laughter.

That evening Rupert led us to Peary's signpost. Rupert's passion for the history of Arctic and Antarctic exploration was to be the source of great comfort and enjoyment during the weeks which lay ahead. The battered signpost marked Peary's final assault on the Pole 80 years earlier. I followed the line of its rigid finger and pondered what Peary, that most ambitious of men, had thought while standing at this point. His black companion, Matthew Henson, had been there with him but there were no monuments to his memory. I glanced at Darryl's feet and just hoped.

Beneath the signpost there lay a small ammunition box in which Peary had left a message from Amundsen. It has since become tradition for most expeditions to leave a message in this place. Rupert, Graeme and Darryl had deposited one the previous year during their May reconnaissance.

That evening, our final evening, as we turned to go back to camp, we were engulfed by the most beautiful sunset. The bright pink orb rolled gently beneath the frozen sea beyond Ward Hunt Island and the mountains which guarded our camp glowed pastel. After dark, a

37 Peary's signpost – little had changed in eighty years

38 Graeme reads out a message from a previous expedition

voluptuous full moon hung above camp. Rupert ski'd down the hill and along the beach to gather his thoughts. For him this moment was especially acute and I found myself regretting the gulf that had grown between us these last few months. Rupert had given three years of his life to see us here together now, gazing upon a landscape most of us had only imagined. This last year had been very difficult for him. He did not like change or unpredictability, and the rapid-fire growth of a project he had helped to conceive had not often met with his approval. Sometimes we had gone for weeks at a stretch without speaking – he infuriated by my lack of accountability and practical application; me irritated by his inability to assert himself, to assume control, to include himself. If there was one thing I had learnt from the very wise and very successful Japanese gentleman, Shingo Nomura, it was that people must not wait to be asked, to be included, to be consulted – they must include themselves and fashion their own place in this world.

As I watched Rupert skiing along the frozen shore I began to recall the years we had shared in some very strange places and I was happy to see his small figure trailing away across the snow, gathering inner reserve, to share another with me now.

The Polar Haven looked like a lollipop. Inside the orange air was hot and putrid. There were almost 20 men, including a television film crew, photographers, the Japanese journalists and base camp team, crowded into the tent. The film director lay in his thermals under a bunk reading a book, ignoring the mayhem which swirled about him. There were microphones, cameras, food, equipment and a constant chorus of 'Who's got my . . .?' or 'Have you seen the . . .?' John Tolson, our cameraman in Antarctica, was a reassuring sight amid this chaos.

We continued the process of weighing and jettisoning equipment begun in Iqaluit. From what we could see of the complicated conditions ahead we knew we needed to travel as light as possible. Six of the team members were to adopt the backpack/sledge combination recommended by Misha. Two small plastic children's toboggans were to be bolted together to form a reversible capsule and the total weight of some 60 kilos was to be divided evenly between these sleds and the pack. Arved and I were going to haul the entire weight in our large boat-shaped sledges. Because we were both much bulkier than the other men, I was concerned that a pack would severely disturb our balance, making us more prone to falls and possible injury.

Misha worked late into the night completing the final adjustments to his skis and clothing until he felt 'personally ready for travel'. He had wired a portable ECG to his chest three days earlier to prove he

39 The last meal together in the Polar Haven

was not above taking his own medicine before he began dishing it out randomly. After his exhaustive medical tests in Ottawa, Misha harboured several reservations concerning the team's health. Beside frostbite, Darryl had an allergic skin condition which would be irritated by a lack of bathing. He also suffered from asthma. Misha thought Arved's lungs were weak and worried about the effects of hotel and airport life on my ability to deal with the cold. Rupert had a very low body fat ratio; only Angus seemed the epitome of fitness, and already he was astonishing us with his ability to cope so easily with the cold. Graeme and Arved had also been weakened by a strange stomach virus during one of our reconnoitres in Iqaluit. Graeme had been forced to return to town; Arved struggled on, vomiting and not eating for several days, through those same conditions which had wrought frostbite on others.

So we were not fulfilling Misha's idea of a perfectly healthy team. Nevertheless everyone was strong; everyone seemed prepared and everyone was, I thought, confident in our ability to work as a single unit.

The morning of the 20th dawned cold and clear. This was it; one chance; last chance; no refunds; no turning back. Our equipment was laid out on the snow by the Polar Haven and we began to make ready. Rupert showed Crispin how to sample for levels of mercury. We all helped Iwata and Akiyama-san, from the *Yomiuri Shimbun*, to launch a

40   The team launches the first of several balloons to test for ozone depletion

large ozonesonde. The huge white balloon rose quickly into the sky, measuring for evidence of ozone depletion as it climbed. The diligent and charming Iwata-san planned to launch several such balloons while in the Arctic, and his results were to be correlated with those obtained separately by NASA.

Medicine, science, movie-making and packing swiftly consumed the morning. Darryl worked silently at his small sledge. The hospital had told him he should not set out; I had suggested he join us on the first resupply flight; Misha had said that, as a doctor, he could not allow Darryl to begin but, as a friend and fellow traveller, he must leave the decision with Darryl who had spent two long years preparing for this expedition. But, Misha warned him, if he received further frostbite injury to his toes he would lose them. The decision was Darryl's and Darryl's alone. All we could do was to pledge him our support.

Stephen struggled to make radio contact with Jeremy at Resolute and finally managed to do so through Fiennes' camp at Ward Hunt Island. When all seemed ready we retired to Polar Haven for a final farewell lunch. It was a jovial affair, as we relished the warmth and a sense of vague normality for the last time. At the end of the meal I stood and said with a dramatic flourish – for if any one moment occasioned a dramatic flourish it was now – 'Well gentlemen, I'm going to the North Pole. Is anyone coming?'

I had looked forward to this moment in many ways, treating the prospect as others would a holiday: no telephones, no airports, no boardrooms, no knives and forks. Yet standing and staring at the sledge and the hated harness, in a temperature of minus 45 degrees celsius, I realised I would rather have been somewhere else a little warmer. I had been through it all before. It felt like re-sitting an exam. I felt that old numbness descending again, like a blanket, as it had three and a half years earlier when I turned away from Scott's hut and headed south. Here I stood, contemplating another desolate expanse of ice. After the interminable, backbreaking whirl of the last 36 months, this was the lonely point of departure. I could feel the sting of the harness, the legs screaming for a chair, the dry cold forging through hot lungs and the sameness – the dull day-after-day sameness – of the world we were about to enter.

The team was strong and good humoured, and they had shown great resourcefulness in overcoming the many cultural and linguistic barriers we carried with us. All the same, I could sense a feeling of frustration and impatience rising among the more experienced men, and I hoped this undercurrent would not emerge to divide or disrupt the team.

Suddenly I wished more than ever for the simplicity of our three-man South Pole journey. Without radios and with limited supplies, that had been a much simpler affair. We either made it or we died. This time we were eight, a large and diverse group. We would carry radios, giving us the option of resupply and rescue if need be. And yet, strangely enough, the fear of failure and the urgency of survival seemed more real now than it had three years ago. There was more to lose. The kids, the environment, my family, supporters, the team, me. There were so many people I would let down if I pulled out. We had to make it; there was simply no other option. I couldn't possibly come back without the Pole. That was the way I had to think; it was the way we all had to think.

Running through our mental checklists, we each fiddled clumsily with Karabiner clips and zippers in the excruciating cold. Physically we were ready; mentally nothing could prepare us for what lay ahead. Even the most confident among our group looked nervous.

Eventually we stood set – 60 kilos per man; ski poles drawn; visors

down. Hasty goodbyes were bid to men of the base camp and film crews. I kept my final farewell for my friend John Tolson. He had been there to see me off to the South Pole: it was so important to see him there now. 'If we did it then, Captain, we can do it now,' I said as I hugged him. He smiled and I turned again, this time to face a frozen sea.

The cold gripped me then, like a vice. Even the sun appeared frozen. The indomitable pack ice reached from the horizon to our feet. I don't think any of us felt afraid, or excited. I didn't feel very much at all. You're not meant to feel anything. You can't feel anything. Because, if you do, it's going to hurt like hell. The body is clever; it shuts down all systems. Feelings don't run that high. There is no thought of fear; only of shutting out the cold; of making one's boots just that little bit more comfortable; of survival.

I turned to Arved and said: 'How are you?'

'Okay,' he replied.

With our large sledges we looked like the heavy brigade dragging the cannons; the cavalry pawed restlessly in front of us.

Our departure, finally, was inauspicious. We were just eight red dots traipsing north.

We fanned out like sledge dogs, pushing off quickly. The small base camp team stood at the top of the narrow ice shelf and watched us forge out on to the pack.

Our tones were hushed. We had stepped out together. Misha would guide; I would encourage; Rupert would navigate; Graeme would humour; Arved would be solid; Gus would ski; Hiro would be organised and Darryl would be there – all the way.

41 *Previous page*: 'An inauspicious departure'

5

FIRE IN THE TENT

The problems began almost immediately. From the moment we took our first steps it was like a bad dream. After turning our backs on Cape Columbia at 3.17 p.m., we crossed the narrow ice shelf which lay between Ellesmere Island and the ocean.

'This could be the only bit of downhill skiing we'll enjoy in 414 miles,' Graeme quipped.

The ice shelf dropped smoothly for half a mile to our first obstacle. The pressure ridge zone had been taunting us for two days now, and as we drew nearer it grew to fill the entire horizon. From here I felt I could almost see the Pole, the whole journey spread before us like a map. But distances in the Arctic are deceptive. The lack of dust in the atmosphere means you can see many tens of miles across the ice fields and fissured glaciers. Vision seems almost too perfect. There is no middle distance, just a blur of textureless white – nothing against which to measure length and size. It was like looking out of an aircraft at high altitude, and as we entered that fractured desert of ice I felt very small.

This was my first encounter with Arctic pressure ice. Rupert and Graeme insisted it was not as bad as they had experienced the previous year during their short reconnaissance, but this news was of no encouragement for most of us. As we began to tackle the great wall of ice in our path I was filled with a dread that this would not be the mere gut-wrenching slog of the South but something far tougher.

It was like Everest reduced to rubble. We scrambled out into the mess, stopping and starting, waiting for others to clear ice ridge after ice ridge. Squinting the ice from my frozen eye lashes, I watched Hiro carefully edge sideways up a snow-covered ice block before tumbling in a tangle of equipment down the other side. We found ourselves on hands and knees clawing up and over the countless razorback escarpments, passing sledges from one man to the other.

'This is terrible work,' Misha muttered. 'It seems to me team in big

73

42 'Everest reduced to rubble'

disorder'. My only light moment was remembering what Christopher Robin had noted during his 'expotition' to the North Pole: 'That's what an expedition means. A long line of everybody.' On our first day we could not manage even that.

Misha had quietly suggested he should break trail for the first three or four days of the journey as he was the most experienced Arctic traveller in the group, but the team would need a strong skier to bring up the rear. Gus agreed that this place should be his. Misha, who had trailed behind for the duration of the Polar Bridge expedition, knew the importance of having a strong man at the back to help the slow and to guard against the weak straggling too far behind the remainder of the team.

So this was the order of things for an hour or so: Misha at the front,

Gus at the back, and everyone else jumbled in the middle. But two hours after setting out Misha looked round to find Gus right behind him. The champion skier in Gus just could not allow him to plod along at the back, so we continued on our way in a haphazard manner, the rear taking care of itself.

The snow was glaringly bright and the whole thing seemed unreal. Was this another training trip? I brushed the frost from my nose. No, this was it, a voice in my head replied. There was far more snow than we had imagined, it was cold and soft, waist deep in places, and grasped at our legs like glue. My large sledge kept sinking like a stone into the white powder. It made skiing incredibly arduous. I cursed Misha for being right yet again. It was easy to understand why Fiennes, hauling almost three times as much as us, was forced to turn back so soon.

43 Hiro straddles a large crack in the ice

We managed only three fifty-minute marches that afternoon, although march seems a rather noble description of our unseemly scrabbling. Towards the end of the day we were forced to cross a line of large pressure ridges without skis. Misha climbed into an ice hole to take photographs of us passing overhead. Without skis there was a great deal of stumbling, falling and cursing. I tried hard to smile for the camera.

When we established camp in the shadow of a large pressure ridge that first evening we discovered we had lost seven litres of fuel – the fuelcan lids had not been screwed on tightly enough. It could have been a very expensive mistake. Misha, already peeved that we had not included the Soviet stoves on the first leg of this journey, was adamant we had enough fuel to see us through the first week. Even so, that would be enough only for cooking, not for heating the tent and drying our clothes.

It was minus 50 degrees celsius, this was our first day on the ice, we had travelled less than three miles, conditions ahead looked grim, and Darryl was suffering from frostbite. To have to retreat to a frozen tent every evening would have been disastrous for morale at this stage of the journey.

We discussed whether to send for more fuel. Misha shook his head disapprovingly. He was concerned lest others should hear our radio plea for assistance, for he did not want the world to know that in less than one afternoon the expedition had landed itself in trouble.

'Safety is our first priority, not pride,' I told him. 'The entire journey lies ahead of us; why take unnecessary risks at this stage?'

The others supported my decision and we sent word to Crispin.

Two tents were pitched – the large Soviet 'horse barn', as we called it, and the smaller three-man 'cottage'. Darryl and Rupert opted to sleep in the smaller tent. They took one stove with them and after supper prepared to settle down for the evening. As it turned out, nothing was ever quite that simple.

44 First night's camp

The Headmaster (as I nicknamed the tirelessly tyrannical Misha) insisted that all four stoves were needed to heat the large tent, which in fact had room to sleep everyone cheek by jowl. So he marched across to the smaller tent without warning, grabbed the fourth stove and returned it to the horse barn. Rupert and Darryl did not utter a word as Misha strode back across camp muttering to himself. Eventually they came across to join the team. Then Darryl and I decided to brave the cold, escape the crowd and sleep in the small tent regardless. I preferred to be cold and alone.

The night was full of spectral beings. A full moon floated in the milky sky above the retreating battalions of ghostly ice pinnacles. Occasionally a wisp of candyfloss cloud floated across the moon, the only movement in a world that was as still as a painting. It was easy to understand why Mary Shelley took Frankenstein's monster aboard a ship trapped in the Arctic seas. Through the surreal mists which enveloped us it was not difficult to conjure visions of Ancient Mariners, of creaking ghost ships, of the soft padding of a polar bear's approach, or the ghosts of Franklin and his men who surely prowled the frozen sea.

Beneath me I heard a groan or the hiss of water escaping through knife-sharp fissures. I slept uneasily, cocooned within the many layers of my sleeping bag. The full moon filled us with foreboding. Misha urged us on before the spring tides could do their worst.

✳

Arved, the first to be on breakfast duty, slept in. He struggled awake – it is impossible merely to arise from a sleeping bag at 8 a.m. in a crowded tent at minus 40 degrees. Much to his chagrin, Misha could not be angry with Arved because he, too, had slept in. The first day had been more wearing than any of us had realised.

Crispin and our photographer Mike Beedell ski'd out with the additional fuel we had requested and joined us for breakfast. Day Two and already I was sick of the food. Crispin reported that all was well at base, where they had received a visit from a lone wolf and completed another successful ozonesonde launch in conjunction with Alert Weather Station. Radio contact had also been made with Resolute, allowing Ottawa Headquarters to receive its confirmation that the entire team – including Darryl – had departed for the Pole.

It was midday before we set out. The weather was clear and calm, with visibility of at least ten kilometres, the mercury down to minus 45 degrees celsius. The all-pervading cold gripped us. No clothing is absolute proof against it. The insulation value of cold weather clothing is measured in 'clo units'. A business suit has a rating of one clo, while the traditional Inuit winter outfit of caribou and seal skins has a value of between eight and twelve units. At the sort of temperatures we were sleeping in, the body needs to be wrapped in about twelve clos. If you are physically active in the same temperature, you need only four or five. As we hauled we sweated, and the sweat froze against our skin as hard as armour. It was an eternal struggle to ensure the cold did not turn to frostbite. We had to think differently about every single thing we did. Everything took longer and every action – the removal of a glove, the adjustment of a boot, or having a pee – needed to be planned carefully. In the extreme cold you become totally attuned to your body and soon gauge how many separate moves are required to complete even the simplest task.

I found it hard to cope with this first full day on the ice. The whole team was strung out erratically again. Hiro, who had been so agile and swift on the training trips, now hung back. With our heavier sledges, Arved and I frequently found ourselves joining him. Misha and Graeme strode out ahead, but the group was widely separated and did not make more than a mile in an hour.

'Never I have seen such bad conditions,' Misha conceded. It was small consolation.

The problems of hauling through deep soft snow were compounded by miles of rough ice and countless steep sastrugi – snow ridges built by winds laden with ice particles.

45 Each man had to claw, tumble and haul his way across never-ending ice ridges

At the close of the fifth march I could see everyone was tired. Darryl and Hiro looked close to exhaustion. I conferred with Rupert and Arved and we decided we should make camp there and then. We had travelled perhaps six miles.

Misha was astonished.

'Why we stopping?' He looked from one of us to the other.

'Because everyone is tired,' I replied.

Misha was furious. 'But you must be tired, this will be normal working situation. Principal position is to move quickly as possible while weather holds.'

He turned to Hiro, who was the most obviously exhausted, and asked him if he was tired. Hiro nodded, but said that he would continue.

'Okay, let's take a vote,' I said impatiently.

Only Gus supported Misha's stand. Misha was beside himself with anger.

'You like children, you are very weak men,' he spat. 'During training session you all heroes, but they only words. If you continue like this we not reach North Pole. If you continue like this I will go to Pole alone and reach it in twenty days. I alone will represent Icewalk.'

It may have been that Misha was trying to arouse a sense of indignity in order to spur the team on, but he succeeded only in alienating and offending most of his companions.

For many of us, this was our first experience of the Arctic ocean, it was minus 45 degrees celsius and everyone was whacked. If we had persisted for another two hours we might have made another mile but would, in my judgment, have lost all remaining enthusiasm for the task. I had learnt from Roger Mear on the South Pole journey that it is very important to ease oneself into these things, both physically and mentally. Three or four miles the first day, five or six the second, while each of us adjusted to the life or death routines required to endure and survive such a hostile environment.

As it was, Misha had come off the ice less than twelve months previously. In many ways he was still a cog in the well-oiled Polar Bridge machine which had rolled on across the Arctic for ninety days. He wanted that machine back again and was impatient with our unease and clumsiness in a place which made him come alive. It was difficult for him to comprehend many of our western ways. He could never understand why I wanted to sleep alone in a small tent. The large tent

46 *Previous page*: Misha had never seen such bad conditions

47 Drying clothes proved a difficult task

was intolerably over-crowded. Every time one person moved, we all moved.

When finally we had all crowded into the one tent there were more 'discussions' concerning who was responsible for what. We peeled off our damp clothing and suspended it from the tent's now humid ceiling to dry. It was not long before we discovered that there was not enough heat to dry our outer jackets. In fact they became only damper as the frost melted and failed to evaporate. Sometimes we left them outside to freeze, scraping off the hoar frost in the morning with a lavatory brush. Each man had come equipped with his own. Misha turned his kamiks (seal skin boots) inside out and let them freeze so he could prop them under his head as a pillow.

*

It was Gus's turn to oversleep next morning. After a rather confused and noisy breakfast we broke camp and struck out again. More soft snow, countless steep sastrugi. Hard and dispassionate, the rough ice protruded like jagged and broken glass all about us. We had expected pressure ridges, certainly. The frozen ocean is made up of countless thousands of ice floes – some only feet across, others hundreds of miles wide. These floes are jostled and propelled by the ocean currents and when they collide they are forced into the air to form long and often steep ridges. Nearer to shore, as we then were, the ice is pushed against the coast, crumpling up on itself. We had expected the pressure to be

48 The team threaded like beads across the ocean's surface

difficult, but we had also expected the ice pans between these ridges to be flat and easily negotiable. This was not to be. In 1989 the atmosphere was filled with ionospheric disturbances and the ocean's surface was one mass of razor-sharp obstacles which forced us to wend and weave our way across the ocean, following Misha's lead.

The day was beautiful, cold but clear. A sea of sun, Misha called it. Hiro travelled very slowly, which puzzled Misha.

'Why you go so slow?' he questioned.

With his head down, Hiro told him that it was as fast as he could go. An accomplished mountaineer, Hiro was none the less unused to carrying heavy weights for such sustained periods. He felt he must pace himself.

Gus and Graeme were adapting to the conditions very quickly and followed hot on Misha's heels. Arved retreated into his thoughts and into his ice-encrusted beard.

On the evening of 22nd March Gus and Graeme slept in the small tent, the first sign that they were to become a mini-expedition. I joined the Headmaster and his boys in the Soviet tent. Misha tried to instigate some sort of system but soon gave up.

With everyone trying to clamber into their bags at once an elbow in the eye was the least you could expect. Misha and I labelled the procedure the 'last march'. Having reluctantly joined the throng on this evening, I established my territory and began wriggling into the three separate layers of my sleeping bag. The first, a plastic vapour barrier, was crinkly and cold. Then I struggled into the inner sleeping bag, and finally into the outer bag. There was little room to move in this frozen straitjacket. I had a small tunnel through which to breathe, but was careful not to fall asleep with my face exposed to the cold air and wake with frostbite. My breath hardened and froze in this tunnel and then dripped back on to my face all night long.

When everyone had finally crawled into their bags the tent looked like some sort of reptilian incubation chamber. We resembled six fatted slugs surrounded by the steam of our breath, shivering like jelly.

The morning of Thursday 23rd March almost brought the expedition to an abrupt close. Misha was the first to smell danger.

'I awake with strange sensation and cannot understand why,' he said later. 'I think it maybe the stoves. I look at my watch, 5.15 a.m. I stand up to brush snow from sleeping bag because it melts when tent becomes warmer. May be better to throw bag outside. When I emerge from sleeping bag I see terrible picture. In place of kitchen I see big fire and in middle of fire I see Darryl. With big effort he try to lift side of tent. In several seconds he manage this and push the stove outside. Darryl follow closely after stove but leave another fire behind. His sleeping bag on fire, also his sleeping mat.'

I awoke to a *whoosh*! and the sound of flailing limbs. Oh shit, I thought, fire. Tent fires are one of the greatest hazards of Polar travel. After Darryl's spectacular exit we were left with a gaping hole in the side of the tent lining. Fortunately it had not penetrated to the outer skin.

'Well, we have eight or nine tent panels left,' I said. 'If we have one fire a week we should just about make it.'

The stove at the centre of the inferno was, naturally, one which Misha had advised against. It was a particularly difficult gadget. In the extreme cold the flanges on the pump contracted and it had to be held against the body to thaw. After this particular incident Misha was determined to reinstate the Soviet stoves.

From the beginning, the stove saga had been incredibly fraught, but then stoves were our very life source. Misha knew the models he had brought with him from the Soviet Union had a problem. They were volatile monsters, spraying fuel in all directions and exploding with monotonous regularity. At the same time, it could not be disputed they threw out far more heat than their western counterparts.

After the fire was extinguished, we had the usual revolting breakfast of muesli, pemmican and hot chocolate and were on our way. A small wind had sprung up, giving a venomous sting to the cold. Exposure to Arctic cold for a few seconds in calm conditions will do no more than give you pins and needles. Let there be just a hint of a breath of wind, however, and you are in for an experience to remember. The wind sucks heat from your body by constantly changing the air around it, greatly increasing the feeling of cold. Icy winds can transform a moderately cold temperature into one of bitter intensity. This is known as the windchill factor. You're not in the Arctic long before you know a lot about it. With windchill, a 30 mph wind can reduce a temperature of minus 35 degrees celsius to minus 70.

Some of us wore huge fox hats given us by Misha. Fur and animal skin were the best defence against extreme cold. Earlier explorers had paid little heed to the Inuit's caribou skin pants and jackets, seal skin boots and fur hoods, and suffered the consequences. They saw nineteenth-century western man as the pinnacle of human development, with nothing to learn from the 'savage' Eskimo. Although the Eskimo survived well in the Arctic, this was not to be taken as an indication that

49 Supper was not always to everyone's liking

his furs might be preferable to regulation navy uniforms. Franklin and his men strode into the Arctic wearing top hats.

All the same, no matter how well prepared you are, there is nothing that is a match for the Arctic cold in the morning. The mucus in my nose froze. If the wind was up the water in my eyes also froze. Vaporous breath was caught in beards or on chins and formed huge unsightly lumps. In these temperatures skin froze to metal, and contact with something as innocuous as a zipper tab could result in frostbite. According to one authority, a common frostbite injury among military personnel was produced when a man's private parts came into contact with the metal zipper of his trousers. Plastic shrank and all foods and liquids were frozen solid. Hot drinks began to freeze while you were consuming them. Pen ink became a solid mass, batteries died and it would take more than five minutes to light a candle because the wax was too cold to melt. If you exposed your fingers to the air they would be frozen in five seconds.

The only way to keep the intense cold at bay was to march all day. Marching made the body sweat inside its layered space suit. The body is a furnace. Even standing still it uses around a hundred watts of power, obtained from food calories. You can boost output up to ten times that by the sort of physical activity we were undertaking. If the

50 Breath froze into icicles on beards and balaclavas

body is kept on the go, its core will always be warm – even if legs and arms are chilled. If not, then the body itself takes over and provides more power through shivering. A basic rule of Arctic survival is: if there is a job to be done that requires physical effort, it pays to volunteer. Once you are on the move, however, things become more complicated. Wrapped in the finest clothing that modern technology can provide, on a bitterly cold day, your armpits are running with sweat within minutes. Having started out well zipped up, you have to unzip a little to let some heat out. The moment you stop for a rest break you have to close up again, trapping residual warmth now that you have switched off your generator.

*

On 23rd March we entered the shear zone and encountered our first drifting sea ice. The shear zone is where the more or less immovable ice crumpled against the coast meets its moving counterpart propelled by ocean currents. In effect the zone marks the edge of the continental shelf. The area was incredibly rough, all ice blocks and very little snow. The team continued to thread like beads across the ocean's surface. Our ten-minute breaks dragged into thirty, then forty and finally fifty minutes as the team waited for the slower members to make up ground. Waiting was never easy, but in minus 46 degrees celsius it made for cold stamping feet and frayed tempers. Despite this, we managed to average six or seven nautical miles a day, which was good considering the conditions and the team's inexperience.

We pitched camp and Hiro did the cooking – a long and not altogether successful experiment. Misha hovered in the background proffering advice. Pointing and frowning, he tried to explain to Hiro that the filth we were to eat should be added to cold water, not hot. I myself did not believe the buckwheat could be rendered edible, no matter what *cordon bleu* procedures were adopted. Hiro and Misha crouched over the pots for a while but to no avail, their conversation revealing a third and deeper language barrier. Hiro had the most wonderful and quirky sense of humour and he was always the first to spot a joke. Misha continued to make attempts to communicate with his Japanese colleague on a deeper level. We all worried about Hiro. We never knew if he were cold, unhappy or tired. There was no hope of teaching him how to cook.

Graeme managed to make radio contact with base at last but the cold was playing havoc with the bank of batteries. Communications were severely curtailed. Base struggled to pass on information obtained from

51 Into the shear zone at the edge of the continental shelf

the most recent satellite photographs.

A frozen ocean is subject still to tidal movements and currents, as we could hear and feel, and the strongest tidal movements occur twice a month after a full or new moon. On 23rd March we were told by radio that these tidal fluctuations were causing some dramatic movements of ice. In less than twenty-four hours an enormous lead of water had opened, a massive 1,000 mile-long gash running north west to south east. It was many days ahead of us, and might cut across our line of travel. There also appeared to be a good deal of tidal movement within our vicinity.

After supper Misha opened surgery. Graeme had a cold and a rash, Arved a deep blister on his foot, but Darryl was in the worst shape. The young American had trailed at the rear of the group for most of the day. His toes gave him great pain, the injured areas having dried and turned black. Darryl was clearly in distress. He was still trying to come to grips with the fear of losing his toes. The tales of Peary, who had lost toes from frostbite, fashioning metal insoles from pemmican tins to protect the stumps of his feet, had taken on a depressing reality.

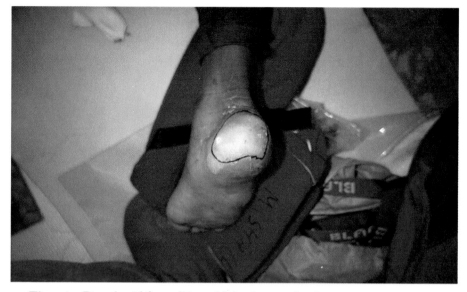

52 The price Darryl paid for walking with inadequate insoles

We had taken a huge risk in allowing Darryl to set out in the first place. Darryl's toes probably would have been amputated as a matter of course ten years ago. Misha was not confident that Darryl could guard against further injury.

Now Darryl had another problem. He had complained that afternoon of a burning sensation in his right heel. Misha peeled off his sock to discover the biggest blister he had ever seen. The doctor was astonished that Darryl had not stopped to investigate this pain earlier in the day. His ski-bindings had obviously been rubbing against his heel. Misha opened the blisters and then bandaged the wound tightly.

6

THROUGH THE PAIN BARRIER

'Let's be honest with ourselves,' Graeme said. 'It's time we trimmed some of the dead wood from the team.'

We were four days and twenty-two miles out from land. The Australian's comment sounded loud in the stillness of this empty place.

That wedge, the almost imperceptible unrest I had sensed in Cape Columbia, had found form sooner than I expected. Sure, the team was still quite shambolic, but it was finding its feet under the most trying of conditions. Graeme's proposal for the slower members to be flown out on the first resupply if they failed to pull their weight was met with a heavy silence.

I saw the sadness in Rupert's eyes and the anger in Arved's. Yet it was a reasonable comment: Graeme, Gus and Misha were working harder than most, both on the trail and in the evenings preparing camp. The team was not pulling together as efficiently as it could and travel was slower than we could afford. We had set out two weeks later than planned and those expeditions which had departed a week ahead of us had managed only twenty or thirty miles in eight days. They were travelling with dogs and snowmobiles. We went on foot. We would have to make haste, but I was sickened that the very essence of the expedition's quest should be questioned now.

This morning we had not cleared camp until 11 a.m., the morning's march had been slow, and the group was strung out over an enormous distance. Those in front could not afford to lose sight of those at the rear and were forced to wait endlessly in the biting cold, losing valuable body warmth and precious time.

Gus was the champion skier. He had prepared for a race to the Pole. This rambling caravan was not what he had expected or bargained for. Graeme was a keen-eyed bundle of energy. He seemed to be everywhere at once, pitching tents, speaking on the radio, lighting stoves, constantly urging everyone to do everything faster.

I understood their sense of urgency but deplored their lack of compassion. Darryl was young, inexperienced and injured; Hiro was small and in a strange land where no one spoke his language. Arved and I were slowing progress with our larger sledges.

'The point is that we were a team when we set out, and a team we will remain until we arrive at the Pole,' I said. 'Not seven, six, five or four of us, but eight. Eight men – even if we have to wait for the slow, even if the journey takes fifty days and not forty, even if we are forced to haul the injured the last hundred miles . . .'

I was upset. Icewalk was a demonstration of international co-operation and strength; this Polar journey was a symbol of what was required to save our world from the environmental threats it now faced. That was why we were all standing about in minus 38 degrees celsius, our arguments freezing solid like cartoon bubbles between us. That was why the United Nations flag was with us, and that was why twenty-two students would gather in Eureka in less than a month's time. It was not primarily a race. At least, not yet.

I wanted to tell Graeme that I understood his frustration and sense of urgency, but I didn't. His attitude offended me. It offended the whole expedition. For us as well as him, the stark realities of the place we now inhabited filled every second of every day. The priorities of survival, and dreams of the Pole – of arriving, of finishing – dominated all our waking moments and guided our actions. It was not a question of 'to the victors the spoils'.

'We are a team,' I said simply. 'End of story.'

We set off again without further discussion. From that moment the group moved a little faster, but I knew some damage had been done. A hairline fracture had appeared in our superstructure, and my only hope was that the crack would not become a rift.

Good Friday, 24th March, saw a lowering of my spirits. The wind was stronger than yesterday, stronger than on any of the previous days. I kept the hood of my windproof jacket drawn tightly about my face. I ski'd slowly, leaning into the harness. Occasionally my mind drifted, but a jar of the sledge would always bring me back to my physical world, a small white oval ringed with fur.

I was thirsty and hungry. Hiro's breakfast had been a disaster. He had, unfortunately, taken one cooking tip too many from Misha; he had mixed pemmican with muesli.

The good doctor struggled to find words of encouragement for his protégé. 'It is special dish with special taste,' he observed, his tone particularly accented.

Graeme and I got some down but our stomachs revolted. Arved would eat none of it, and went instead to check the fuel supply. Our guess had been that about thirty litres remained – six litres per day until the first resupply in five days' time. How could our calculations have been so wildly mistaken?

'There are only ten litres in total,' the German cried in disbelief when he returned to the tent.

'We manage,' Misha said with an air of finality. 'Two litres per day, 250 millilitres per man. Enough to cook, not enough to dry clothing.'

I recoiled at the prospect of five extremely cold, wet, uncomfortable nights, but there was nothing we could do about it. We had no alternative but to press on.

Next day we ski'd by some spectacular pressure ridges that soared 20 metres into the sky. The colours inside these fractured structures made me dizzy – blues of the most surreal hue, like gems, but richer and harder. The imagined faces in the rubble still mocked me, but now they also spoke, groaning as the ice rocked in its watery cradle.

The sun throbbed behind a shifting curtain of haze.

'Pollution,' Rupert said. It seemed the Arctic Ocean was becoming a soup of chemicals. The haze we could see now was industrial effluent.

I remembered Will Steger's account of his 1986 venture. At the

53 Harsh ice conditions slowed the team's progress

Pole, he wrote, 'they excitedly filled us in with news from the outside world, principally the explosion at the Chernobyl nuclear power plant, which had happened just the day before. They informed us of the radioactive gas cloud in the polar jet stream, which had passed directly overhead. How ironic, to be in so remote a place and yet face such risks.'

If exploration had shown me one thing it was that the world was a very small and terribly vulnerable place.

We had survived the morning's crisis of confidence and after a brief break pushed on hard. Suddenly Graeme collapsed. He lay where he fell, not moving.

Misha called out to him: 'Why you lie there?'

There was no answer.

Misha ski'd over to the prone Australian and felt for his pulse. Still he did not move. He lay in silence for several minutes. The doctor looked concerned, but did nothing save monitor the pulse. Eventually Graeme groaned softly and stirred. He was completely exhausted after working harder than most and battling against a serious bout of bronchitis.

'We must all pass through threshold of pain or exhaustion,' Misha said 'Then worst is over.'

Our camp that evening was surrounded by pressure ridges. Like a flaming, crimson ball suspended from the northern heavens, the sun suffused the sea ice with its glow, turning the jumble of ice blocks into soft marshmallows.

Cooking was always a loathsome chore. Misha coaxed the stoves to life, tending carefully to the pathetic whimper of a flame which was so slow to gather any strength. Supper took two to three hours to heat up in the small battered pots. The hot milk Misha prepared that night was especially comforting. It even put a smile on Darryl's weary countenance.

'Hot milk good for stomach and spirit,' Misha pronounced as he shared it round. His simple action had drawn us more closely together.

After supper I prepared a bed in my sledge outside. The temperature fell to below minus 50 degrees. I crawled into my three layers of sleeping bag and settled into my unorthodox nest. Staring out through the narrow tunnel to the sky above, I decided to smoke a cigarette. Unfortunately I had forgotten the matches. I could hear Misha fossicking about outside the tent and called to him.

54 Pressure ridges soared as high as 20 metres

Misha grinned down at me: 'I am Russian doctor, and as doctor I am not able to help you smoke, but as your friend I must help you.'

He repositioned the cigarette in my mouth and lit it. We grinned at each other.

Glasnost.

I lay there feeling as though I was adrift at sea in a small boat. Somewhere, not so many metres beneath me, water was lapping at the underside of the ice. I smoked my cigarette slowly and realised how lucky I was. I had the support of the best people, I had a wonderful team and dedicated back-up. We had turned a one million dollar debt into a four million dollar expedition in just over twelve months and we were on our way to the North Pole. Even so, I couldn't clear my mind of the suspicion that once again disaster could be lurking just round the corner.

I remembered as a teenager returning from a holiday in Greece, having blown all my money on wine and a girl from Rhyl called Wanda, and being desperately in need of a quid. Ian Blenkinsop, a local builder and character of some distinction, handed me a ladder, explained the finer points of gutter cleaning and told me to start knocking on doors. Standing atop my ladder one day, and leaning heavily to my right to clean a corner gutter, I over-extended myself, the ladder fell away from beneath me, I grasped on to the gutter and brought the entire structure down on my head. I fled the garden in fright, and so ended a promising career. So it went on, culminating with the loss of the *Southern Quest*

55 *Previous page*: The sun softened the ice's savage beauty
56 The team rested for ten minutes every hour

57 Drifts of soft snow hampered progress for the big sledges

minutes after Roger, Gareth and I had achieved the South Pole. Endless weeks lay between us – at 83 degrees 30 minutes north – and this other Pole and I was wondering again what setbacks lay ahead. As I drifted into sleep icicles of breath plopped on to my face.

An early start next morning saw us on the road by 9.20 a.m., promising to put the 'go-for-it-boys' in a good mood for the rest of the day, never mind our damp clothing. Hiro's was almost wringing wet. In the haste he lost his lavatory brush, and before long my ski-bindings snapped. Everyone was then forced to stand around in the cold for an hour and a half while we lit a stove, warmed the glue and screwed the bindings back into place.

We moved off again. There were deep drifts of soft snow and I found my sledge almost too heavy to haul. I had rarely been so demoralised wading through snow as glutinous as porridge, step after step, mile upon mile. I comforted myself with the thought that the experts said the first 120 miles were the worst.

To break the tedium I tried to work out which distant figure was which. Already I was able to identify people, no matter how small a dot they were on the horizon, by their walk or gait, by their equipment or stance. These things were like a person's fingerprints – the way they stood, the way they moved, seemed to voice something of the inner man.

Misha was very solid. His skiing style was strong – not fluid, almost a form of marching. Gus looked as graceful as a cat, skiing with a rolling, elegant motion, completely effortless. It was as if he were waltzing in a straight line. Graeme was often hunched over, and usually looking down – quick, but purposeful. Rupert had textbook style, very professional, but he, too, was crouched over, his neck elongated like a tortoise's as he strained against the weight of his sledge and pack. Often the load on his back appeared to have complete control of his small frame as he teetered in one direction or another. Hiro wobbled about like an old man, his head always down as he followed Misha's trail. He never looked up, as if he were absorbed in some private ritual. Darryl was all over the place. He had some serious problems with his skiing style, and was not being helped by the injuries to his feet. His gear shifted wildly in all directions as he persisted in trying to walk rather than ski. Arved was very upright and very consistent. I have no idea how I appeared, probably a mess.

Towards the middle of the day we stumbled across some polar bear tracks. Angus unslung the rifle he carried in case of attack, but pronounced the tracks to be about a week old. I was relieved. The largest carnivores in the world, polar bears are fearsome hunters in an ice kingdom where they are quite clearly king. They roam the ocean in search of seal, and explorers report sighting tracks as far north as the Pole itself. Occasionally they invaded my dreams as monsters. A tent

58 The expedition was armed in case of polar bear attacks

would provide precious little protection against one powerful swing of a paw.

That evening Misha found a large, flat ice pan, maybe two or three years old, on which to pitch camp. Graeme's bronchitis had by now deteriorated into raging 'flu. Poor guy, he had been suffering dizzy spells all afternoon but hadn't said a word. Skiing in a mental fog, he had at one stage crashed into Darryl's sledge without seeing it. Now his nose was running like a tap; it must have hurt like hell in these temperatures. Darryl was faring little better. Frostbite and blisters gnawed at his feet; every step registered pain.

It had been a very broken day, only six hours of travelling, and this evening the cold was particularly bitter and telling. As we struggled to erect the tent, the cold nailed my hands through my gloves and I thought: 'I hate this.' Even Misha admitted that conditions were 'a little chilly'.

My hands still hadn't thawed properly when it came for me to cook supper. I wrestled clumsily with the stoves and one of them leaked fuel on my bare fingers. I almost screamed with pain. I was convinced I would get frostbite.

My curses were a reminder to Arved that he should check our fuel levels again. He made another alarming discovery. Our fuel reserves were down to less than four litres. The emergency can was inexplicably empty, and the resupply plane was not due for another three evenings.

We were in real trouble. This time we had taken it to the edge. We could not afford to move on, not in these temperatures, not with Darryl in his condition. I could not ask people to march without food and without fuel. I could not gamble with their lives.

'We can't go on,' I said.

Graeme supported my stand. Only Misha wanted to press on, but it didn't take much to persuade him that the situation was too dangerous.

'We'll call for an early resupply,' I said. 'Until it arrives we must wait.'

And wait was all we could do – in the freezing cold, adrift on a frozen sea. Wait, and pray.

7

TIGERS AND DARK HORSES

One bank of radio batteries had seized in the cold. Even if we did make contact with Cape Columbia we wouldn't have long to speak. Graeme turned the dials with his numb, aching fingers and eventually Stephen's measured voice crackled out across the emptiness.

'Advance Base to field party. Can you copy? Over.'

'We copy you, Stephen,' I shouted into the frozen mouthpiece. 'Listen, this is not, repeat not, an emergency, but we have been struggling with cold temperatures in the forties and below and we think the fuel cans have either cracked or the seals have cracked. Do you copy? Over.'

I waited for Stephen's faint reply, then hurried on, fearful of losing the batteries or of the signal breaking up.

'We are going to remain in this position until we can receive resupply – in other words air supply. I say again, this is urgent but *not* an emergency . . . the conditions have been rough but we have been pushing ahead very well. This is the Icewalk polar team at minus 45 going clear – 'bye.'

The radio gurgled hollow before fading into silence. We would be fine provided the aircraft could find us. If the weather closed in, the Twin Otter would be grounded in Resolute or Eureka – and in the Arctic it was not unusual for planes to be delayed for many days. In these temperatures, without food, water or heat, it was difficult to know how long we could hold out.

Water is the main problem in Arctic survival. Because the air is so cold, it cannot hold moisture. It is therefore very dry, which means that the body loses as much as a gallon of water a day through the nose and breathing passages as it automatically humidifies the parched, incoming air. The result, if you don't take in a lot of fluid to counteract it, is dehydration – a greater problem in the Arctic than it is in the Sahara, because for some strange, physiological reason your body does not make

59 Graeme talking to advance base

you feel thirsty in the cold. By the time you *do* feel in need of liquid, you are dangerously in need. It's a vicious circle. A 2.5 per cent loss of body water results in 25 per cent loss in working efficiency, yet the more you dry out the less thirsty you feel. Fainting and heart attacks are common in the Arctic; you have to force yourself to keep taking fluids – but not in such large quantities, Misha would contend, that you hinder the body's ability to adapt.

Just to make matters worse, you tend to urinate more in the Arctic, especially during the first few days after arrival. The cold makes your body shut down peripheral blood vessels in order to preserve core temperature. The blood therefore flows in a smaller system, your body senses that there is too much fluid and starts to get rid of some in the form of water. In ordinary conditions water loss makes the blood saltier, so you feel thirsty and replace the lost fluid, but in cold regions the salt is excreted as well, together with potassium, both of which are needed to keep the nervous system and muscles ticking over properly. All this lost moisture has to be replaced, and it takes a lot of snow to make just one pint of water. We were boiling 12 pints at a time, and that takes a lot of fuel. Rupert's calculation was that we could survive for twenty-four hours in a vapour barrier bag without liquid. We still had enough fuel to melt a little snow, but that was all.

It was a hellish day-and-a-half's wait. We stayed in our sleeping bags to conserve energy as best we could, though mine was full of ice. I had no way of escaping the cold. Graeme sat hunched like a statue, monitoring the radio. We were all hungry and unhappy. The cold had its first real chance to batter us: we weren't moving and we had no stoves, every last source of heat had left us. The risk of frostbite increased one hundred fold. Every time someone left the tent for a pee he returned with frostnip to his fingers. Even when they thawed it was difficult to know for sure that the cold had not taken its irreversible toll.

Everyone remained very quiet inside the tent. It was exhausting, just being. Outside, all was still; there was barely a breeze to stir the soft snow. I lay shivering in my bag. Part of my brain was beginning to long for deep sleep. I felt myself drifting in and out of consciousness. I was running by the river in front of my mother's house. In the summer there is nowhere more beautiful. I was sitting in a whirlpool on the soft mossy rocks beneath the overhanging trees, the cool water coursing about my warm body. The moist, fragrant scent of dusk and a soft trickle of laughter swept out of the darkness to surround me. I could hear the wind and the sound it made through the thickets of trees on the other side of the river.

I stirred and tried to turn over. I wondered if the others also dreamt of warm places. Time inside our tent had slowed. Everything was motionless and dusted with ice. There was slowness in all things. The men looked drugged, sitting or lying perfectly still in the cold, their bodies occasionally racked with a fit of shivering. The cold, a deep, bitter, unbelievable cold, crept into the very centre of my bones and the last vestiges of warmth began to ebb from me.

This was the time of Scott's last march. At this time he would have been lying in his tent awaiting death. I felt closer to him now than ever before. Perhaps it had been as simple for him as drifting off into a sweet dream; perhaps it was a pleasant sensation; perhaps it was a relief. I sighed heavily and stared at the team for some time without really seeing them. I seemed incapable now of coherent thought or action. When they came into focus it was difficult to recognise who they were. After only six days our faces and bodies had been ravaged by the cold. Arved was half the size I remembered him; his nose was a mess of frostbite. Graeme appeared grizzled and coughed alarmingly. Rupert was smaller than ever. Darryl bent protectively over his injured feet; I thought he looked completely overwhelmed. Hiro's tiny dismayed

60 Hiro records another tiring day in his diary

frame seemed to have no chance of fighting back.

During the afternoon Rupert took it upon himself to struggle out to locate a landing strip for the Twin Otter. He found a suitable area around 600 metres in length and spent two hours levelling it, digging out ice humps and marking its perimeters. The pilot would be relying on Rupert's judgment. If the ice was too thin, the strip too short or rough, the plane would capsize or tip on impact. Rupert returned nervously to the tent; he hoped he had chosen well.

Graeme stayed by the radio but there was to be no aircraft that day. The sun slipped quietly from the sky but the light stayed with us. Night was but four hours long now.

A morning without heat or food. My sleeping bag was freezing and I was beginning to feel weaker still in the face of the unremitting cold. I thought I had a touch of frostnip to my thumbs. I paced about, stamping my feet and swinging my arms, trying to warm my core. My fur hat was like a slab of concrete on my head. My kamiks had frozen into an awkward shape, making me shuffle rather than walk. The morning passed achingly slowly as I watched the sky for a sign of life.

✳

Everyone roused themselves sluggishly to greet the distant buzz. We stood like shipwrecked men on a desert island, bedraggled and hungry, staring up at the small aircraft as it circled our camp site several times

61 Logistics director, Jim Hargreaves, delivers the first resupply

and then banked away again. The strip was too short.

The Twin Otter flew on, eventually touching down more than one and a half miles from camp. We staggered through the soft snow, leaving Darryl behind.

'You okay, my brother?' I asked as we left.

'Yeah, I'm okay,' he said dejectedly.

It was a long one and half miles. Hiro stumbled like a drunk, his boots half on, half off. Graeme hobbled; one of his boots had frozen into an unwearable shape. I wore a tent slipper on one foot. Rupert fell into a large open crack in the ice. It was like the retreat from Moscow.

John Tolson, with movie camera, emerged smiling from the aircraft. Dave, the sound man, was with him, as well as Mike our photographer – heavy with 'flu – and Jim Hargreaves wearing filthy banana-yellow trousers and one of Misha's discarded Soviet jackets. His huge laugh bounced out across the ice. John and I grinned at each other.

'How's it going, Rob?' he asked with concern.

'Not bad,' I said. Then I corrected myself. 'Actually, it's awful – very difficult, far tougher than the South.'

'How's Darryl, where is he?' John asked. I think everyone at base expected Darryl to return on this flight.

'He's struggling, but Misha thinks he can go on.' I did not want John to know the seriousness of Darryl's plight. I did not want our people in Ottawa to begin agitating for his evacuation. To the outside world we must appear a strong, cohesive team, despite the split that was developing and the problems that Darryl's deteriorating feet might cause us all.

John did not press me on the point; he just smiled and rolled the camera.

Resupply was like Christmas. We rushed at the mountain of cartons spilling from the plane, hunting about for letters, munching on fresh fruit before the cold could turn it brown. I discarded my ice-caked sleeping bag, and Arved and I exchanged our large sledges for back packs and smaller sledges. We saluted the monsters as they were loaded aboard; perhaps they would be back when the going became easier.

We received new batteries for the radio, more food rations, further supplies for Misha's medical programme, the Soviet stoves and enough fuel to make a proper job of burning the tent down. Poor Rupert was unable to deliver the huge number of snow samples he had laboriously collected. They were too heavy to drag to the aircraft.

An hour after landing the little plane climbed slowly into the sky and we were left alone again. A split-second glimpse of the outside world, then it was gone. It took two long and difficult journeys to return all the equipment to camp.

Some 380 miles lay between us and the Pole – perhaps 500 miles of travelling when the southerly ice drift had been taken into account. Darryl's feet would only get worse; Hiro seemed weakened, as did Arved. I wondered what our chances really were. If we made it, could we make it by 5th May – our target date – in order to meet our students at Eureka before they returned home? It was depressingly clear to me now that it was going to take a great deal longer than the forty days we had anticipated.

So on the seventh day we rested.

✳

The day began with another tent fire. We heard an explosion and a sharp yelp of pain. Graeme had left the fuel cap off the stove after refilling it; he ignited the burner and the flames exploded. He heaved a 12-pint pot of hot water on to the inferno, scalding himself in the process.

Misha tended his minor wounds before resuming his research

programme. He commandeered Darryl as nurse and together they withdrew phials of blood from each of us in turn, chatting about Soviet-American relations while the centrifuge whirred in the background.

'I cannot believe', Misha said, 'black American and Soviet doctor sitting near to 84 degrees on Arctic Ocean, working together and discussing world problems.'

After the bloodspilling the Soviet stoves were marched into action. The first we named Tiger; it roared to life. The second was called Dark Horse, because it took some time to show its true colours. Despite the reservations we held about these temperamental creatures the tent was warmer than it had ever been and we were able to dry all our equipment.

Everyone was occupied – this was to be no indolent holiday. Misha nagged us to be more organised; he deplored confusion. He was angry with Arved; he seemed to have had a problem with Arved from the outset and I couldn't understand why. Now it was the food. He complained that Arved had not organised the food properly for the days of rest.

'It is big disorder,' he grumbled, accusing Arved of not pulling his weight in an area which was his specific responsibility.

Arved said nothing. He always closed down when he sensed anger.

One rest day passed into another. Misha was irritated, Arved quiet and Rupert unhappy. The Royal Marine was receiving little support for his scientific programme. It was difficult work, tackling heavy sampling equipment in these conditions, taking off his gloves to operate unco-operative air pumps. Most of his fingers were frostbitten. He often worked late, and one evening, when he returned to the tent, just a single stove remained burning feebly. Somehow we had forgotten about him. There was no hot food left, and Rupert was desperately cold. Others among us, myself included, would have yelled and cursed but he just quietly withdrew. Rupert never rocked the boat.

The anniversary of Scott's death, 29th March, was a day of quiet domesticity. The sun shone boldly and it was almost pleasant. I thought of Scott – '. . . outside the door of the tent it remains a scene of whirling drift. I don't think we can hope for any better things now. We shall stick it out to the end but we are getting weaker, of course, and the end cannot be far. It seems a pity, but I do not think I can write more . . . For God's sake look after our people.'

62 Misha's medical programme takes priority during the team's days of rest
63 Arved contemplates the next 377 nautical miles

It was 30th March before we began heading north again, although we had drifted seven miles Pole-wards while we camped. Base would be worried by the delay but we had an enormous amount of equipment to sort. Arved and I had to transfer our gear to the Karrimor packs and small Norca sledges. The beleagured tent was in need of repair, and the food needed weighing, packing and allocating.

I awoke at 6 a.m. Still prone in my sleeping bag, I grabbed my hat and hunted around for some gloves. I blew on my fingers and then tucked my hands under my armpits to warm them. I quickly brushed away the ice which had formed near the mouth of my bag and then began worming my way out. I crouched near the floor, found some more gloves, my knee-length pile socks and plastic tent boots. I then dived out of the tent with my sleeping bag and rolled it up as quickly as possible before the moisture which had formed inside could freeze.

It was time for my appointment at the 'John'. It was the best time of the day to tackle this problem because afterwards I could return to a relatively warm tent and thaw my fingers before breakfast. It was simply a matter of forcing the body to adapt. If you waited until after breakfast your fingers were frozen; then fastening ski-bindings and adjusting packs were difficult enough, let alone manipulating squares of toilet tissue.

It felt a bit warmer, perhaps minus 35 degrees. I wouldn't need to wear full kit. Three days ago it had been thermals, fleece-lined underwear, a Helly Hansen full length pile suit, a duvet jacket with fur-trimmed hood and a windproof shell, balaclava, fur hat, four pairs of gloves and three pairs of socks. Today, as ever, my kamik boots were frozen solid. If they did so in an awkward shape I had to warm them or force my feet into them and hope against hope that there were no nasty crinkles on the soles to pinch and cause blisters.

While breakfast fermented Misha ministered to everyone's ailments. We sat silently for the most part, feeling stronger after the days' rest. We all hoped the worst lay behind us, that our baptism by fire had drawn to a close. Gus and I emerged from the tent first, as usual. We heaved the canvas from its ski supports, snatching shelter from above the remainder of the team who were still dragging on their frozen boots.

Mornings were times of confusion, everyone wandering aimlessly, brains not yet in gear, not talking a great deal and bumping into each other. Gus, Graeme and Hiro were always ready first. Hiro had a

64 *Previous page*: The days lengthened rapidly: soon the team would march into twenty-four-hour daylight

65 The team is forced to remove its skis and walk

mountaineer's knack with equipment and he seemed to need much less of it than most of us. This particular morning Gus and Graeme seemed even more eager to leave and scowled impatiently while the rest of us fussed about. Misha was terrible this morning, absolutely wild, but then it usually took him an hour or so, out on the trail, to get his head together. His grumpiness this morning was a tremendous relief. We had expected him to rise at 4 a.m. and insist on full drill. To discover that the steel-like doctor was human gave us all hope.

At last we moved off. The small sledge was strangely skittish; it had a life of its own, bouncing at the heels of my skis like a puppy. The ice was not as chaotic this morning but the snow was soft and deep. Ahead lay a large line of pressure ridges.

We spread out as we usually did – Misha, Angus and Graeme in front, the rest of us jumbled behind. Arved trailed the group, often stopping to vomit. Gus had jettisoned his fur hat and was wearing only ski cap and ear muffs. His face was speckled with small flecks of ice; Inuit sweat heavily through their faces, a quirk of evolution which helps to conserve heat. Graeme was pulling two small sledges lashed together rather than one.

'My whole mind is becoming consumed by these things,' he groaned as he ski'd ahead to climb a small rise. As he began his descent the second sledge caught on a piece of ice and he hung there suspended.

66 Hiro battles through soft snow

Throwing himself forward, he tried to free the sledge. It suddenly snapped loose and Graeme tumbled down the other side. The path was strewn with boulders of ice and we were all eventually forced to remove our skis and walk.

As the day drifted away we moved north, slowly shuffling rather than skiing. I began counting my steps and that at least convinced me that I was making progress. There was no other means of telling; for hour after hour, the world around me was nothing but mountains of white. The doubts of the past few days had disappeared. I no longer thought of rivers and of home, but only of the difficulties which lay ahead. I was concentrating solely on the walk, registering each of my steps, trying to pace myself as much as possible. I had no noble feelings or thoughts. I saw only my feet, the next steps, the next ridge, I was moving automatically. I didn't think of the Pole. I didn't think of the team. Only that I had to put the next three yards behind me – that alone was important, and nothing else. A single word went through my mind, and it matched the rhythm of my steps: 'Forward, forward, forward'. Over and over I chanted it, like a mantra. Mechanically, I put one foot in front of the other. That was the extent of my achievement.

Most of us had stripped to just two layers of underwear and a jacket. We paused for ten minutes, which dragged on into half an hour while we ate chocolate and biscuits and waited to regroup. We looked like a snowmen's convention, dusted with frost on our lashes, our hats, our clothes. The fingers and toes were hardest to keep warm; we jiggled about, constantly shuffling from one foot to another, going cross-eyed trying to check that the tips of our noses had not turned white.

Misha and Graeme moved off again. They wanted the group to move fast and Graeme was angry that we were so strung out.

I was finding it hard to come to terms with the backpack. It was hurting, and Arved, too, disliked the change. What was more, he was beginning to feel very ill. We were now only twenty miles behind the Mako and Flowers expeditions.

✳

I shivered convulsively. Misha shaved small, round patches on my chest and then adhered half a dozen electrodes to these areas before strapping the portable ECG around my waist. The last day of March was cold with a strong wind from the north west that drove icy tendrils into us, deadening all sensation in face, fingers and feet. The ECG kept catching on my pack. Misha was taking a battering from the wind.

67 A well earned break

He strapped on a black Darth Vader-style facemask, but it obscured his vision and he went crashing off a high snow bank, hurting his knee. He tore off the mask furiously and carried on, trying to ignore his rapidly freezing nose and cheeks.

The sun had some warmth to it but still the group straggled far and wide, winding in between the huge blocks of ice, each man alone, following the ski tracks in front of him.

Graeme's and Gus's patience had worn thin. They did not want to wait around any longer. Graeme wrote in his diary –

> We've had this really nice approach of 'Now chaps, let's do it for 50 minutes, rest for 10, with 20 for lunch.' It really hasn't been adhered to much at all. So we took the harder line today and just got up and left at the end of each time and people were missing out on their rests. It soon started to sink in and they didn't really appreciate it much. Arved is feeling very unwell but he needs to be up with the group and he spent the whole afternoon by himself with very few or no rest stops.

Arved was clearly ill, but he said nothing and chugged away like an old tug at the back. He was vomiting and couldn't eat. Out here we were so susceptible to viruses. People had been known to catch infection from opening cans of food, and in this cold there was little chance to shake it off.

Darryl's blister was growing larger and eating deeper. He found it difficult to travel quickly. Hiro was struggling, although he couldn't tell us why. Rupert, who seemed to have lost yet more weight from his already thin frame, was gathering strength and moving near the front of the group. Everyone had frostbite. Arved's nose was very badly affected and he was forced to wear a shield. The tips of his fingers were also bitten and beginning to disintegrate. Most of Rupert's fingers had been injured. Misha's and Graeme's noses had not escaped. Hiro's cheek was scorched.

Illness is a lonely affair. We were becoming increasingly isolated as we dwelled on our ailments and retreated into our own thoughts. I needed Misha's support to keep this team together. The moans from those at the front were not helping; the sick needed encouragement.

Despite Arved's illness and our slow tail we managed eight full fifty-minute marches. We stopped to camp on a large flat pan of ice near a wall of pressure ridges. Arved, who was carrying the big tent and most of the cooking pots, was nowhere to be seen. He staggered into camp forty minutes later. The team was cold and angry but no one expressed their feelings at the time. Gus took Misha aside later that evening.

'We must go to the North Pole and not wait for those who cannot keep up.'

Misha said nothing. He knew Gus was homesick.

✳

We had crossed the 84th parallel and our first domino had tumbled. It was April Fool's Day and we had travelled some sixty miles: only one seventh of the journey, but it felt good to have crossed the first line of a map we all held in our heads – even if that map, in my head, looked like a boiled egg, with the Arctic the top that you knocked off with your spoon.

Misha had slowed his pace, allowing everyone to congregate during the hourly breaks. I think he hoped to coax others back into the team and encourage those at the rear into a higher gear without their noticing. Graeme was still eager for the race. I found out much later that he vented some of his frustrations into a dictaphone buried deep within his sleeping bag.

> The team is basically divided into a couple of categories; there is the one going for it and getting somewhere, which are Misha, Angus and myself, and there is the rest who are at this stage like little boys in a big man's world. Darryl has had every single thing imaginable wrong with him, but still going. His frostbite has settled down and he is actually moving but he has a long way to go before he puts in a hard physical day. Hiro gives it a good belt but he is not really on top of it . . . Misha has gone through the stage of being angry with what the boys aren't doing and is approaching it philosophically now. My patience has worn out and is coming around for a second go and I'm starting toward the philosophical side with Misha.

> Gus reached the end of his tether today more or less with the slow skiing and so he cleared off and had a ski around by himself and took a few pictures . . . These guys haven't realised that in order to get to the Pole they have to put in the physical effort and you have to sweat, it's going to be hard graft and it's going to be unpleasant and if you don't do all that then you just aren't going to get there. We still have 360 miles to go and that's a fair way in anybody's book. I mean that's six weeks if we knock over 60 miles a week.

I ski'd near the front for most of the day, with Misha explaining

Arved's illness. We talked of ways of uniting the group and helping the
sick to move faster. I desperately wanted to see the students; to me they
were the most important aspect of this expedition.

The ice was kinder today, though not much. Rupert fell heavily but
was uninjured. I could only hope that conditions would ease as we
neared the 85th parallel and we could make up the time we so badly
needed.

Then we received news from the outside world that made our need
to move faster all the more urgent. Stephen's voice crackled faintly
from the radio. We crouched round the small box pulling our jackets
about us tightly to squeeze out the evening chill. Base camp slowly read
a long message from the director of the television documentary, who
had just returned from Moscow. The Soviets had agreed to press
ahead with building an outside broadcast station on a large ice floe.
The floe would be chosen for its predicted direction and duration of
drift, with the aim of timing its arrival at the North Pole to coincide
with our own. The technique had been used before by the USSR with
a high degree of accuracy, but never as the means of transmitting live
television pictures around the world. If it came off, it would be a
remarkable first. Stephen articulated the message painfully slowly, his
voice disappearing every few seconds into a barrage of static. I craned
closer to the radio trying to catch each broken word.

> If everything goes as planned, the Soviets will need to set up a
> direct radio link between you and Ice Station Icewalk to help with
> navigation and to enable them to pinpoint as accurately as possible
> the date of your arrival. This must be early in May, before the 10th
> if possible. Given Arctic weather patterns this year, the Soviets
> feel they will have only until then before the ice starts breaking up
> and they have to withdraw.

The Soviets were prepared to sink more than two million dollars into
the project; the director had to raise a further one million within ten
days, through the sale of television rights. It was now a matter of seeing
whose task was most difficult, his or ours.

The North Pole has always been difficult to visualise. In the past it
has been depicted as open water, a continent, a dark magnetic mountain. Some Inuit called it the Big Nail, after one of the more useful
items of trade introduced by early explorers. I had never thought of it as
anything much at all. Live television from the North Pole would
certainly ensure the Icewalk message had global impact. We would
have to try harder to be there in time.

68 The pressure ridges eased off, but only temporarily

We were travelling in March and April because the sea is frozen solid, visibility is good and the days increasingly light. By May much of the sea ice begins to rot and becomes unstable and dangerous. Whatever the conditions, you cannot reach the North Pole over the ice in a continuous straight line. Delays and diversions are caused all the time by breaks in the ice. Taking resupply flights into account, we now realised we would need to cover at least eleven miles per day to meet the deadline – not an impossible task, but certainly a substantial one. There was nothing we could do but do it.

The following day was enough to quell our optimism immediately. We had ski'd for only half an hour when we encountered a huge wall of pressure ice. We took off our skis and began to scramble over. There was another great wall. We cleared this, and there was another. Soon we lost count. The ridges were taller and closer together the further north we pushed. At one time we were forced to ferry equipment by hand from man to man over a series of crevasses.

Misha and Graeme were about 100 metres ahead. They climbed on to a large block of ice to scan the horizon. Misha turned to Graeme.

'Beautiful ice, beautiful.'

70 Graeme negotiates a break in the ice

When I joined them I could see nothing but a living nightmare, an apocalyptic vision of huge ice boulders and pressure ridges stretching as far as the eye could see. The sun had swung round behind us; a searching wind began to ruffle the hoods of our parkas.

There was nothing for it: we hitched up our sledges short and pushed on. Men were falling everywhere, our packs taking control as we tried to wend our way between or over the boulders. Hiro, dwarfed by his pack, was suddenly in his element. This was mountaineer's work and he did brilliantly, climbing quickly to the front of the group.

My back was beginning to hurt badly. It was an old rugby injury, aggravated by the South Pole trek, which chose now to re-surface. My kamiks were twisted, too; one of my feet felt colder than it should have done. I hated this incessant scraping and crawling. This wasn't a voyage any more, it was an obstacle course.

By late evening Misha eventually spotted some flatter ice and we made camp. Despite having covered less than six miles, well short of the eleven needed, spirits were high. We had conquered without injury the worst ice Misha had ever seen and were now level with the Mako and Flowers expeditions.

69 *Previous page*: 'Beautiful ice, beautiful'

8

THE GREAT UNREST

The 84th parallel is notorious. Here the sea floor rises sharply, causing dramatic tidal movements and severe pressure ridge activity. The appalling ice conditions of the past few days were symptomatic of a moving force beneath our feet which we could neither see nor feel. The ocean's impact built wall after wall, planted minefield after minefield. It wanted us dead. I was not surprised that the 84th parallel also marks the point where many expeditions have turned back.

Towards the end of Tuesday, 4th April, we felt the character of the ice change. The pressure ridges eased, the surface was smoother under our skis. The horizon seemed to have drawn a deep breath and opened up. We approached a huge expanse of flat ice, the largest we had seen yet, and crossed at its edge. The ice was very thick and hard. Then we saw our first open water, a crack no more than twenty centimetres wide.

We stopped and gathered at the edge of the fracture, staring into the still, black water. Hiro bent to smell the unstirring sea. Rupert and I dipped our fingers into it, withdrew them and shook hands firmly.

We had left the fixed ice and the coldest temperatures behind and now stood on the moving ocean. This tiny crack of black water was like a starting gun to us. The race had begun. Whether 5th or 10th May, these had been artificial deadlines imposed upon a place which would give them scant regard. The first sighting of open water was our real signal to move. It indicated changing ice conditions, warmer weather and the eventual break-up of the ice pack altogether.

The entire team was very tired. Frostbite and flu had taken their toll, but now a sense of urgency crept through us after two gruelling weeks of cold, slow and argumentative travel. We knew it was time to begin the push. We completed nine fifty-minute marches, or 10 miles, on 4th April and this placed us at 84 degrees 22 minutes north. It was not far enough, but given the ice conditions it was as much as could be expected.

The next day Darryl lagged far behind the group. His toes were giving him great pain but it was the blister on his heel that seriously retarded his progress. The wound sent sharp burning pains into his achilles tendon, as if someone had pressed glowing embers against his skin. The ulcerating blisters were not healing, despite Misha's diligent care. For Darryl, each step was more difficult than the last, and we were often forced to wait as he hobbled to catch up the group.

The perpetual twilight warmed my cold bones. As the temperatures slowly climbed into the low minus 30s I began to realise how much the cold of those first few days had enfeebled me both physically and mentally. The warmer temperatures were as welcome to me as the first scents of summer. I didn't think about the nightmares they might spell for the future of the expedition.

Camp was made slowly. Rupert and I were on supper duty; the others attended to their equipment. Misha was on hand with a number of suggestions to help speed the cooking process.

'Relax, Misha,' I told him. 'This is our baby.'

We cooks made a radical culinary decision. We chose not to add milk to the buckwheat, to see if this would render it more edible. Misha peered suspiciously at the green substance in the pot. He was appalled that we could even contemplate omitting the milk.

'We thought people might like to try something different,' I said.

The Headmaster shook his head disapprovingly. 'But this is not right,' he argued. 'If we use milk only in hot chocolate it means not everyone will receive equal share of protein and calories – Arved drinks two litres, Hiro one and I only 350 millilitres each evening. It seems to me we need have milk in buckwheat so everyone, ah, receive equal share.'

Something I did not recognise snapped inside my head and I hurled every ounce of milk into the buckwheat.

'This is my last Polar journey,' I shouted angrily. 'While I am travelling I am happy but when I am in this tent with all these people I am very unhappy. I don't want to be here, we have too many problems and too many arguments.'

Misha collapsed into the armchair he had moulded out of his sleeping bag, a look of bewilderment on his face.

'But Robert, Robert, what are you saying now? You collected us from all over the world into this tent and now you tell us you

71 At last the horizon opened up
72 The first sighting of open water

want not to be here. We are in difficult situation. We must be all
together, but you wish to be separate. We have many problems, but you
as leader have not kept all questions under control. We have chance to
reach North Pole, and many people rely on us. It is bad decision to
change rations, it could jeopardise chances. Milk with buckwheat
maybe – ah – disgusting, but it is essential.'

I knew he was right and said no more. Misha was troubled. Me – I
was angry with my outburst, I didn't understand it. I knew only that
I felt increasingly the need to be alone. Survival is a strange and difficult
taskmaster. Each of us had changed since setting forth on this journey,
each of us had withdrawn a little in his own way. Rupert had said barely
a word for a week, Hiro no longer smiled, Graeme exploded angrily
with the least provocation. I realised that only Misha remained
unchanged. He was all things to each of us – guide, navigator, doctor,
nutritionist, mentor, technical adviser. He was above and beyond
reproach, he shone in this hellish place; it was his territory and he felt
heavily the burden of guiding us through it.

I admired Misha and knew full well that he was the key to our nailing
the Pole. My anger was therefore all the more inexplicable, yet it
burned within me, this childlike sulking, for the next two days and it
drove the team from my side.

73 Concern mounted with reports of large open leads of water ahead

74 The ocean hissed balefully beneath their feet

Gus arose at 4 a.m., disturbed by the sound of moving ice. He crawled outside to check that there was no danger of it breaking near us and splitting the camp. A heavy fog curtained him from the world. Below, the ocean was hissing balefully. Visibility was less than ten metres, but he was able to satisfy himself that all was well – for the time being at least.

Graeme made brief contact with base. Bad weather was imminent. A large low was moving south from the Pole and seemed likely to close in for several days. We had food for only three days, and conditions heralded a radio blackout. I prayed that our second resupply would not be delayed.

A strong south-westerly wind blew at our backs as we forged out into the great white vacuum. The ends of our skis were lost in a swirl of snow, ice walls towered to either side of the horizon. I pushed on across the ridges which criss-crossed our path, often sinking groin-deep into the soft snow. Each step called for a concerted effort, and my back hurt more with each step. As we slipped and slid from the last of these spongy precipices we were met by a broken, moving plain of ice and a large expanse of open water shrouded in thick sea mist. We gathered on the edge of this eerie, seething lake, and watched while Misha tested the crumbling ice, first with his ski pole, then with the weight of one foot.

'Follow me,' he said as gingerly, he began to edge his way across the treacherous surface. 'But please, be careful.'

The ice rocked terrifyingly and began breaking under our feet. We almost danced across the fragile surface in an attempt to keep moving. Fifteen minutes later we encountered more pressure ridges and veered to the left for a quarter of a mile to circumnavigate them, only to be met by more open water. Misha leapt on to a large island of ice and we followed one by one until it began to rock and list dramatically. We scrambled back. Moments later the island disintegrated and sank.

The leads of brackish water continued to the west and were becoming wider. Behind us, where only fifteen minutes earlier there had lain open water, the surface had already frozen and was groaning and pushing into the air to form small ridges.

Misha turned back to the open water before us, took off his pack and sledge harness and very slowly edged his way out on to a narrow ice bridge. We watched, not daring to breathe lest we disturbed the delicate crust. The lead was twenty metres wide, or more. The surface felt firm and Misha motioned for us to follow one at a time, without our equipment. The fog was closing in, there was little if any contrast between ice and sky. We could have been walking on a cloud, the ice beneath as compliant as cottonwool.

We pressed on, huddling closely together like cattle before a storm. Misha led another dangerous crossing, calling: 'Quickly! Quickly!' to those of us at the rear as the ice began to quiver beneath our feet and the fog swirled in tighter. We took shelter from the wind beneath a large pressure ridge and ate a hurried lunch of hot chocolate and biscuits. I was surprised to find myself eating slightly less each day.

In the afternoon Arved's ski-bindings snapped. We had no spare bindings left, so Misha fashioned a substitute with rope, using methods he had learned as a child in his native village of Rjazan near Moscow.

We were very tired that evening as we set up camp. I helped Hiro to heave his sleeping bag into the tent and was amazed by its weight. On closer inspection we found it was full of ice. Hiro must have spent a sleepless week, without any warmth whatever. No wonder he was so weakened. That he had said nothing about it was another example of the language barrier between us. He had become isolated, unable to share in our discussions in the evenings, unable or unwilling even to complain of his plight. I missed the Hiro who had begun the journey smiling and joking, bidding us 'G'day' in perfect Australian. But then this place had made all of us withdraw to a degree.

We located some flat ice for an airstrip. Given the worsening weather and rising winds, it would be prudent to remain encamped until the resupply flight arrived. Rupert, Misha and I built a snow wall to protect the tent from the gathering storm and then hurried back to our sleeping bags to await further news. At 5 a.m. we learnt the worst: our Twin Otter had been grounded in Eureka, and there was no prospect of it taking off soon. We passed the day tending the airstrip and repairing our equipment. Misha bent over one of his many tables of calculations and arrived at the alarming conclusion that we had been travelling at an average rate of 0.8 miles per march. At this speed it would take the best part of another two months to reach the Pole.

'Misha, North Pole in June,' Gus laughed.

'Maybe July,' Misha replied.

Inside the tent we cowered from the snow swirls which had begun a wild dervish dance outside, and talked.

'Arved – ah – where was your father during big war?' Misha said. It was clear he had been wanting to ask this question for weeks.

'He was a doctor working in a hospital,' Arved replied.

'My father was in Soviet Army,' Misha announced. 'It is strange their children are now sitting in tent, working together to survive and discuss world survival.'

Misha led the ensuing conversation with warm enthusiasm. This concept of international co-operation was so new and so real to him that he made the expedition come alive again.

Misha and Arved spoke at length about their respective lives in the Soviet Union and West Germany and the frictions that had existed between their two countries. Misha said later that the discussion had freed his brain and drawn him close to Arved. The ghastliness of the patriotic war still burned deep within the Soviet psyche and needed expression. Outside the storm raged, but in our tent world problems were solved with ease and we all relaxed into the unique warmth that is forged through adversity.

I sat with my back against Misha's, making notes. Rupert was hunched over pages of figures, something to do with the sun and the moon and the drift of the ice. Arved and Graeme were reading. Hiro was trying to sleep. Gus wrote letters. Darryl was restless. He had a lot to learn about just waiting.

✳

Storms in the region typically last three or four days, so base camp had decided to bring the resupply forward by twenty-four hours before conditions could worsen. On Friday, 7th April, they finally received word from the pilot of the resupply aircraft.

'The plane isn't going anywhere – bad weather has hit Eureka, zero visibility.'

The aircraft would be grounded at least a day and a night. The weather in Resolute, too, had closed in, with heavy snow, the wind was gusting to 20 knots, and zero visibility. At least they had managed to get the plane as far as Eureka, which would enable us to take advantage of any window in the weather.

'One day's fuel left and one day's food,' Arved said flatly.

By Sunday the situation would be worrying, by Monday or Tuesday serious. By Wednesday it would be critical. If the aircraft went out and was unable to locate us in poor visibility, the expedition would still be liable for the $15,000 charter fee, though in my mind expense was not a consideration any more. I didn't want to be responsible for the airlifting in a few days' time of eight corpses off the ice.

✳

We ate only half rations on Friday night. The winds howled like the living dead through the ice canyons, skipping and screaming along the walls of ice. They played havoc with the surface of the landing strip, scouring it in places. Sea smoke shrouded the horizon, indicating more open leads of water nearby. I felt that truly, no place on earth could be more exposed.

Graeme stayed with the radio almost through the night, and was finally rewarded with the news that the pilot was going to chance it. The aircraft was on its way.

The Twin Otter appeared from the mists low over the ice. It came down heavily, bouncing wildly to a skidding halt. The flight had been difficult and the pilot had landed almost against his better judgment.

John Tolson emerged from the aircraft, looking shaken by his ordeal.

'It was a pure coincidence we found you,' he shouted into swirling snow. 'The weather has been terrible all the way. We should never have landed. We came close to smashing the plane.'

We unloaded in a hurry, the pilot accelerated up the short strip, and in seconds the plane was swallowed up by the white-out.

After floundering back to camp we began immediately to dry our equipment. While Hiro's sleeping bag thawed out, the discussion

75 Sitting back to back, Misha and Robert write their diaries
76 On half rations, the Polar walkers await resupply

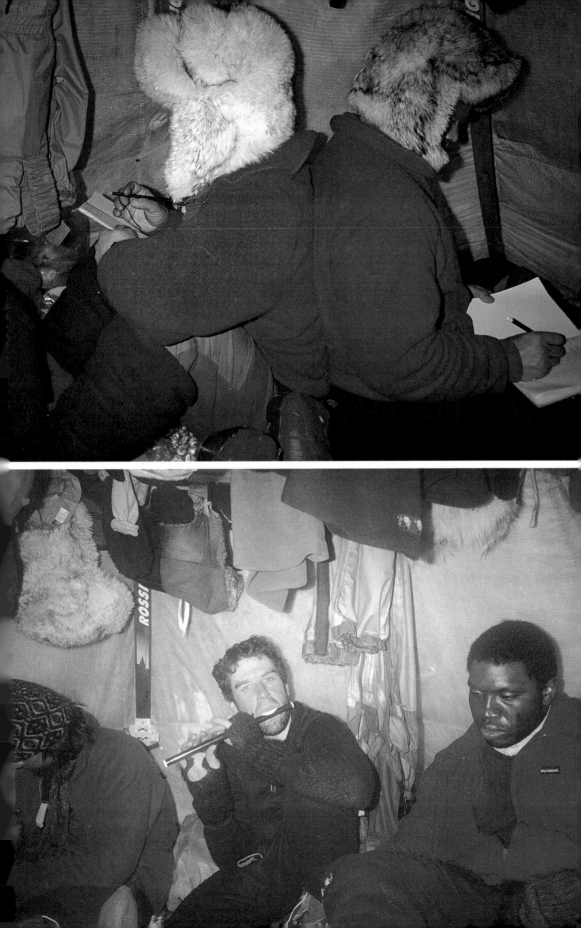

77 A Twin Otter of Bradley Air makes its final approach

turned to ways of travelling faster. We had fallen far behind schedule. If we were to encounter more weather like this, and the attendant open leads of water the warmer temperatures forebode, then we would lose any chance of meeting the Soviet Ice Station at the Pole.

'Why don't we reduce our rations to eight days' food and nine days' fuel?' I suggested. 'We could travel much faster with the lighter weights and schedule one extra airdrop of provisions, which shouldn't delay us by more than half a day.'

Misha agreed. 'We have not been hungry,' he said. 'But it is a big risk.'

An airdrop would be an easier proposition for the pilots of Bradley Air. Our landing strips had not been good. Expeditions on skis are notorious for selecting poor landing sites because they never cover as much ground as dog teams, which range widely among the pressure ridges to find a path, and therefore have more opportunity to select suitable terrain. On skis one tends to press ahead on a selected bearing.

I spent our day of rest alone in the small tent, reading letters and scrawling in my journal, the tips of my fingers so numb I could not feel the words I was writing. It was minus 42, but we were relieved that the temperature had dropped and hoped that the open leads we could sense by the cold smoke on the horizon would now freeze over again.

For the first time on this journey I felt comfortable enough within myself to think about something other than our own immediate needs. I had been jettisoned into a world of ice, my head full of fears and concerns which belonged to another existence. Out here every minute of every day had been focussed upon how to climb this obstacle, negotiate that sheet of broken ice, straddle this open lead. As I lay there in my sleeping bag I drifted off, my mind freewheeling over the struggles of the early travellers and my explorer predecessors, over centuries of Arctic legend. Since 825BC, when the Greek Pytheas is supposed to have sailed as far as Iceland, there have been many tales about the cold land 'without all hope of day' at the end of the Earth. Whalers, sealers and beaver hunters played an enormous part in exploring the area. I knew from my days of studying history at Durham University that commercial motives also prompted early desires to find a passage from the Atlantic to the Pacific. Bering, the Danish explorer who discovered the eponymous straits, was sent by Peter the Great to see if a land bridge existed which would connect Asia with North America. The vision was clear: a trading route across the top of the world, a shipping lane north of America to the fabulous riches of Cathay, the Orient. The way was unknown, unmapped, and its defences were formidable. But for centuries men were to argue, to search, to suffer and to die in the attempt to trace this route that was known only in myth: the North-West Passage.

The search led early explorers into unsuspected terrors, into seas and lands of a hostility beyond their belief. Seas in which mountains of ice swung irresistibly, towering cliffs whose sudden thunderous collapse of ice could entomb men and their ships, lands so barren that it seemed nothing could endure but cold itself. Yet men did endure.

The hardships were awesome. Expeditions whose vessels lay splintered fought their way back overland, scraping meagre lichen from the snowbound rocks, chewing leather, surviving in cold so extreme that axe-heads shattered on trees frozen to granite. Against the elements at their most vicious they pitted human endurance and a ruthless ingenuity. In the teeth of disaster the search went on.

The story of that search links immortal names – Cabot, Frobisher, Hudson, Ross, Franklin, Nansen, Peary, Amundsen – in a saga of unequalled endurance. It is a story of feats of navigation, of exploration, of speculation, of heroism, of greed, of survival. Above all, it is the story of an idea that possessed the mind of man and outlived all the tragedies, the torments and the ironies of the long quest.

The Arctic must have had a special magic for the early voyagers, an

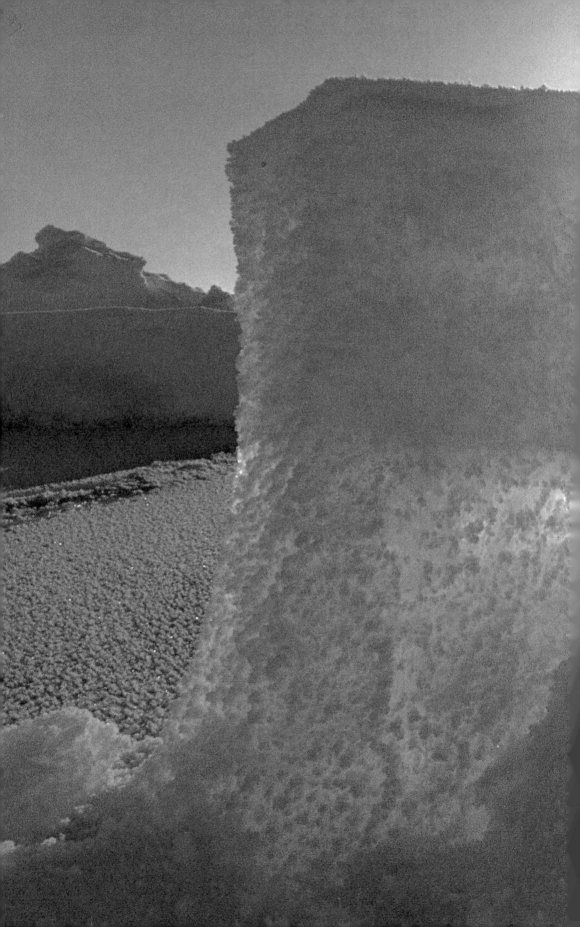

irrestible magnetism that drew them on. To be the first man to set foot at the Pole presented a particular kind of challenge to a particular kind of man – of courage, endurance and fortitude. Other explorers had to contend with disease and hostile populations. Going for the Pole was more of a straight fight, one that appealed especially to men whose single-mindedness compelled them to set aside all other considerations and concentrate every effort on one specific goal.

In the 1860s and 70s an eccentric American called Hall embarked on a series of expeditions which culminated in him briefly holding the record for 'farthest north'. But the record was grasped at the expense of his ship and his own life, and his death was perhaps one of the factors which led Karl Weyprecht, in 1875, to deliver an address to the German Scientific Association in which he made a plea for international co-operation in Polar research. There was far too much emphasis on spectacular feats of exploration, he said, such as reaching farthest north or being first at the Pole, whereas what was needed was teamwork and unbiased research. Weyprecht's words struck home, and 1882 saw the first International Polar Year, an event which finally led to the international attempts at co-operation of the present century, including Icewalk.

✳

I had a bath in the morning, being the only team member mad enough to join the good doctor's hygiene programme. We melted pots of snow, took off everything except our tent slippers, dashed outside, washed and then dived back into the tent before our extremities could freeze. The entire process was masochistic but prevented the skin rashes and irritations I had loathed on the South Pole journey.

The weather remained cold but the storm had passed. We could feel the ice and snow conditions changing again as we travelled; the snow was harder and the skiing easier. It was Monday, 10th April, and we were beginning the third stage of our journey.

The mechanics of moving, of staying warm, of staying alive still dominated my consciousness. It had been quite different three years ago. Then I had had months in a small hut in the winter's darkness to prepare myself for the voyage ahead. I had seventy days and seventy nights of sameness, marching three hours at a time, nine hours a day. It was a journey into a great white void and a journey into myself. I was free to roam the world in my mind.

78 *Previous page*: It is easy to understand why the Arctic held a special magic

79 Arved Fuchs: 'I voyage'

Apsley Cherry-Garrard said that exploration is the physical expression of an intellectual passion. It is also a great unrest. From the moment I met Arved I knew we shared this sense of travelling. Lumbering behind most of us at the rear of the group, he had embarked, not on a race to the Pole, or a flag planting extravaganza, but something far more personal. He once said to me that painters have only one way of expressing themselves, they paint.

'I have another way,' he confided in me. 'I voyage.'

I found Arved's attitude a source of strength. Rupert's also. His passion for the history of Polar exploration and his dedication to science gave this journey a deeper purpose. To get to the Pole was not enough for him, it was a piece of ice much like any other.

I was sure that Graeme's and Gus's impatience had been increased by their nightly isolation from team discussions, but on the evening of 10th April the entire team slept in the one tent for the first time. Misha was delighted. Surely as a team we would learn something from our struggles, and it was only as a team, without malice, that we would prevail?

I remembered something that Bruce Chatwin, one of the travellers I admired most, had written about the great unrest:

As a general rule of biology, migratory species are less aggressive than sedentary ones. There is one obvious reason why this should be so. The migration itself, like the pilgrimage, is the hard journey: a leveller on which the fit survive and stragglers fall by the wayside. The journey thus pre-empts the need for hierarchies and shows of dominance. The dictators of the animal kingdom are those who live in an ambience of plenty. The anarchists, as always, are the gentlemen of the road.

For this particular group of gentlemen, the journey was poised to become a race. Misha extended our working day. We would have fifteen-minute rather than ten-minute breaks but march eight one-hour sessions rather than attempt nine fifty-minute marches. This system worked well on its first trial, the extended breaks allowing more time for the team to regroup, even though it was not an easy day. The temperature had dropped and a strong wind had stirred. The ice was thin and precarious in places and broken in others. We could feel the ocean beneath our feet today, the drift was strong. We staggered into camp that evening like a field finishing the Grand National, our heads low and our gait so laborious that Misha held his breath lest we collapsed before finishing.

80 Extended rest breaks allowed more time for the team to regroup

It was late. I lay vacuously contemplating the fact that more people had scaled Everest than had travelled on foot to the Pole. Misha was mumbling into his dictaphone in Russian. A strange noise began to penetrate my drifting consciousness. It sounded for all the world like the tread of a very large creature circling the tent. I glanced at Misha as his hand reached silently for Gus's rifle. He slid a round into the breech and stood up.

'Bear,' he whispered. I opened the tent flap a fraction for him and held my breath as the brave Soviet doctor first watched for signs of movement, then slipped out into the darkness.

Suddenly I was wide awake, heart thumping. No sound could be heard save that of steady breathing. My eye fell on the rifle where Gus had left it in its case. The Russian was not in his place beside me. Could I have been dreaming? Or was he out there lying stunned, maybe dead, where the great white beast had cut him down? I was filled with dread, and felt unable to move to investigate. At last, as my resolve returned and I stirred myself to leave the warmth of my bag, a heavy crunch of ice outside the thin tent wall only a few feet away sent a shock through every nerve in my body. I braced myself to meet whatever it was . . .

The tent flap flipped back and the Russian stumbled in. I stared at him while he settled back in his former place. The 'bear' was Darryl, on the prowl for something to eat. The relief mingled with acute anxiety. Was I so far gone that I could hallucinate the whole frightful scene? Was this my submerged and secret terror? I wanted to purge it from my mind – and maybe I did just that, for recalling the fierce emotion of it now I cannot be sure that any part of it really happened.

9

A FRAGILE BRIDGE

We were hungry for news of the miles that had fallen but, without radio transmission, were unable to receive our satellite co-ordinates from base. Rupert tried to fix our position with the sextant but failed. So, on 12th April, we set off again, with only the previous day's compass bearing to follow, and without knowing how far we had travelled.

Graeme and Gus were the first to depart camp; the rest of us caught up with them half an hour later as they waited near a small ridge of broken ice. We walked along this feature until we ran up against pack only a foot thick. Misha guessed this place to have been a great sea only days earlier. The area of thin ice was almost two miles across. To the right, dark vapour clouds stretched to the horizon above open water.

The clouds were rolling in our direction. To the left, the large sheet of frozen water was contained by a long string of pressure ridges. The ice was criss-crossed with small leads of open water, sometimes covered by the flimsiest skin. Open water barred our passage to the right. If we moved straight ahead, there was a risk of stranding ourselves on an island should the ice begin to break up.

'We have no choice,' Misha said. 'We must march straight ahead.'

He led the way. I brought up the rear. After twenty minutes we were drawn up short by the loud clash of breaking ice. It was a fresh lead. The ice was moving swiftly, colliding with some force.

'Hurry, hurry!' Misha cried.

We crossed, but immediately came upon another small river of open water. We followed this to our left for some time, then waited while Misha scouted ahead.

Rupert took a sextant reading. Minutes later Misha reappeared, shouting to Rupert to pack away his instruments. The ice float was

81 A tiring mixture of broken ice and deep snow
82 Vapour clouds stretch to the horizon above open water

beginning to break up, and unless we moved quickly we could be cut off from the main pack and set adrift. Now almost running, we charged between the open leads, balancing on the spongy ice. Those in front leapt across a small gap with one stride, the edges crumbling beneath their feet. Arved and I followed at the rear with our large sledges so as not to risk destroying the fragile bridge over which we crossed one at a time.

Misha halted again, this time before a lead no more than ten paces across, covered with a plank's thickness of ice. It was a living thing, closing gradually while we watched. The newly-formed ice crawled on to the surface of the approaching pack or disappeared beneath it. Tongues of brittle grey advanced on us steadily. Misha started searching to the left for a place to cross. Suddenly he waved his ski stick. The tenuous ice field had come to an abrupt end. With relief we moved back on to the thick pack. We had been literally skating on thin ice for almost two hours.

The weather began worsening as soon as we had gained safer ground. A strong wind blew from the north east into our faces. Misha's nose and cheeks became frostbitten, and it grew ever colder as the afternoon wore on. Hiro staggered near the back, looking very weak.

At the day's end Misha stood to announce that we had completed 480 minutes of travel that day. Everyone cheered.

'It is brilliant!' Misha exclaimed. 'Polar expedition record.'

Though exhausted, we all felt a sense of elation. The team had found itself at last, and had shown that a system for survival could emerge through adversity.

'We can make up lost miles now,' Misha added, smiling wryly as he realised the influence his slovenly friends were having on his meticulous thought processes. He had never used the word 'miles' before. But miles seemed so much more evocative than minutes or kilometres of the vast distance still to travel.

We pitched camp near a small band of pressure ridges. Dark clouds were gathering on the horizon and a menacing dusk settled heavily about us. We erected the tent hurriedly, Graeme and Gus assembling the frame, then helping Misha to drape it over our skis. The rest of us worked quickly to shovel snow around the base while Graeme laid the floor. Hiro and Arved refuelled the stoves while Graeme and Misha ignited them. The fuel was still causing some problems and the stoves had to be cleaned every three days.

Outside the storm raged, but with four stoves burning the crowded tent seemed a warm and safe place to be. During the day Misha had taped the sounds of the moving ice; he played them to us that evening.

83 Firing up the stoves

They sounded alien and far away in the humid warmth of our shelter.

Hiro was close to exhaustion. It was difficult to know what was wrong, so isolated had the language barrier made him. Eventually we discovered that his inner sleeping bag was very damp again. He was obviously very cold at nights and barely sleeping at all. I suggested that Hiro should sleep between Darryl and Misha; I would take his place at the edge of the tent, where it was much colder. Hiro, who had never complained, agreed to my suggestion with smiling alacrity.

The radio blackout continued. Base must have been extremely anxious. We were unable to receive our position but continued to activate our Argos satellite beacons every evening, hoping that Jeremy knew where we were and that we were safe. This theoretical safety net was of little comfort to us, however, as the storm blew through the night and into the following morning. The air was thick with snow, and I could trace only the barest outline of the nearest pressure ridges. The winds seemed to be coming from frozen hell itself, pouring between the ridges of ice which protected us and crying out across the open plains.

Misha was unsure if we should set foot into this maelstrom. The batteries were exhausted. Graeme was still unable to make contact with the outside world. We had now been cut off for three days and had no accurate way of knowing where we were, or even if base had managed to keep track of us. We decided to continue North, for time and tide were against us, and in my mind the North Pole was fast receding

84 Struggling across an open lead

again, beyond an increasingly watery horizon.

We packed up quickly as the wind roared about us. I pulled my hood close to block the storm from my ears. Bags and equipment flew about camp and we ran crouched into the white wind, snatching up things before they threatened to disappear into the ocean's frozen vortex. We pushed out in a line. By lunch, conditions had eased a little, but the Grand National had recommenced.

Gus and Misha were confronted by an open lead some three metres in width. The channel was brimming over with water and ice. The lead's edges were grinding together as Misha and Gus stood and watched. Misha shouted for us to hurry while he hunted for a place to cross. The ice began to crack, the sound ricocheting out across the emptiness. The small floes were forced together, one climbing and sliding atop the other. The flat section of ice chosen by Misha for our crossing was being forced vertically into the air. There was really nowhere else to go. Misha prepared to climb up on to the plate of ice and slide down the other side but at the top he waited for Hiro who was trailing far behind the group. When he caught up, Misha yelled for us to follow. As he uttered these words he went crashing down the plate of ice, the cold, death-black water lapping up from beneath to meet him. He flailed to his feet, the ice grinding all around him.

Misha was unhurt and, after a short breather, thought it tremendously funny that he had called us to follow him falling down. Even so, obviously agitated by his near miss, he ski'd over and said firmly to Hiro in English that even he would understand:

'Hiro, you must go faster. You say, you not tired. Me, usually tired. You walk behind, I go ahead. I make way for all. I do very hard job. Now you do same. Do not fear. Tiredness, common state at end of day.'

Misha then hastily put on his pack and ski'd away without waiting for any of us. We followed in silence. Misha believed we each had to push ourselves to the limits of our physical endurance and, having crossed that threshold, move on unshackled by the chains of tiredness. He desperately wanted Hiro to cross that barrier with us, but I think he regretted his angry outburst.

'Some of the team need to be spoken to in that way,' Graeme and Gus reassured him later.

They urged the doctor to have similar words with Darryl, who was now lagging far behind the group. Misha refused, saying Darryl's feet did not allow him to go faster.

I gave Arved and Rupert the tent. 'You go ahead,' I told them, 'I'll stay with Darryl.'

The two of us walked into camp half an hour behind the rest of the team. Darryl was limping badly. Misha had prepared tea; it reminded me of Christmas Day with Roger and Gareth in Antarctica. After supper Misha examined Darryl's feet. He discovered the American had been walking without proper insoles – equivalent to marching in bare feet. His blisters had been rubbed raw. Misha beckoned me over to inspect the disturbing wounds. We both scolded him for being so

85 Darryl's injury got worse by the day

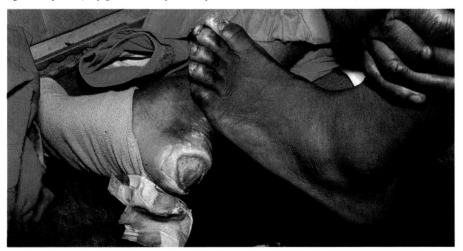

careless and inattentive, but he had probably been too tired or pained to notice. Inwardly I was concerned. The heel of Darryl's right foot was beginning to look like a cross-section of fresh steak.

∗

We had crossed the 85th parallel but did not know it. That evening I lay in my bag and thought of the students. I conjured up a vision in my head which allowed me to follow the progress of us all. I reduced everyone to small flashing red lights on a military map. There were eight red lights bleeping towards the Pole; twenty-two others, in fifteen different places from Sydney to Beijing, bleeping brightly around the world. In my mind's eye, the twenty-two dots began to move towards Canada. I had visited almost every country included in the student programme and could visualise their individual voyages. I could sense the temperature as they left home. I had memorised the world time zones so I knew whether it was dark or light. I could see the airport terminal and remember the colour of the lounge chairs. I knew how long each flight would last. As these little dots bleeped northwards I imagined the students' nervousness and excitement. I thought about them gathering and meeting in Ottawa, clambering aboard their Bradley's charter flight, and eventually the Twin Otters. I could follow each and every journey and this gave me a great deal of pleasure.

The importance of the student expedition was never far from my mind as I huddled in our battered tent. These students took Icewalk from being just something to being something special. We were engaging young people in a fight to protect their own future. I think only Rupert shared my deep pleasure in these thoughts, for his love of the Polar worlds was going to be shared by them, and after three years of thankless slog, that made him very proud.

I was sad that I could not be there in Eureka with them, and as the weather outside grew grey again it seemed increasingly unlikely we would be at the Pole in time to greet them.

Lying there in my sleeping bag, I considered the dedication of my companions, the work and effort they had contributed just to get this far, however far this was. Yet few of us had considered the efforts our young friends were making at this time to prepare for their first encounter with our frozen world. All I had done to rehearse for this

86 Classroom in the cold

87 The students conducted their own tests to determine the level of ozone depletion in the Arctic

expedition was to drink a few litres of muscle-building milk drink, visit a gymnasium once or twice when my schedule allowed, and run occasionally.

In Kenya Stanley Gachui was walking many miles each day carrying heavy weights, swimming countless lengths of the Starehe Boys Centre swimming pool. He was doing star-jumps, squat thrusts, press-ups, trunk curls, sit-ups, mind sharpening exercises; he was huddled in a cold room, studying mountaineering and survival books; he was learning his knots. For Stanley was preparing to board his first plane, leave his hot country for the first time, and fly into the Arctic Circle.

In Australia Emma, Danny and their guide Wendy slept the night in a deep freeze, the press in full attendance. In Canada Peter talked his way into a McDonald's board meeting and five minutes later walked out with a cheque for one thousand dollars to help fund his participation. In Northern England Mike was being mobbed by girls on a train bound for London after his first television appearance. In Brazil Anne lost her nerve before her television debut but the result was an overwhelming response to her commitment. In London absolute pandemonium broke out when the Duke of Edinburgh's Award Scheme officer realised that the Indian student Shailendra had gone missing. They found him two hours later rowing on the Serpentine: after hearing tales of Stanley's training regime he had panicked and dashed off for my style of eleventh-hour work out.

The idea of the student expedition had taken form as I flew over Northern Ireland on my way to Belfast to deliver my first Duke of Edinburgh's Award Scheme lecture. I remember gazing out of the aircraft at the beautiful countryside below, as richly green and fecund as the Arctic is dazzling white. It was difficult to relate the simplistic beauty of what lay below to the reality of the conflict in Northern Ireland. I thought, you only ever hear bad news about Belfast, let's give them some good news for once. Despite the urgency of Icewalk's environmental call to action, I did not want to be another prophet of doom; ours was a story of hope.

Colin Henderson and Eric Rainey, who had enthusiastically lobbied for me to address the Northern Ireland Chapter of the Award Scheme ever since it had lent its patronage to the expedition, choked on their Guinness when I suggested that what the expedition needed was a

88 It wasn't all hard work

89 The students and their escorts: 'We are the problem, and we must be the solution'

Catholic girl from Belfast. 'Furthermore', I said, uttering the idea as it occurred to me, 'I'm about to go to Dublin, so why don't we include a Protestant boy from the Republic of Ireland?'

We knew it was right – a strong, evocative and symbolic beginning to the student expedition. Icewalk's underlying ethos was bridge building; the bringing together of those separated by the arbitrary barriers built by their parents and their parents' parents.

Why not kids from Northern Ireland and the Republic? And why not kids from Hong Kong and China, the United States and the Soviet Union, Brazil, India, Japan, West Germany, Kenya, Australia, New Zealand, Portugal, Canada and England?

Colin Henderson loved the idea and soon became one of the expedition's most enthusiastic supporters, convincing a group of Belfast companies to establish a CFC (chlorofluorocarbon) recycling plant. In Hong Kong, Chinese-speaking student escort Chris Lonsdale was organising environmental awareness exhibitions. In Japan, Makoto and Tomomi were writing articles for the *Yomiuri*'s giant junior press division. In Michigan, Michael was doing likewise for the Booth Newspaper Group. There were countless people everywhere, working hard to make the expedition a success.

While I stared at my clothing, drying as it dangled from the top of the tent, I realised it was nothing short of a miracle that the students were about to set out at all. It was such a relief to know, as we trudged across the 85th parallel, that everything was going ahead according to plan. As I drifted into sleep, I tried to ignore the dull ache near the base of my spine.

10
WAR OF ATTRITION

I thought we had seen the worst of it, but the Arctic had yet to put up its toughest resistance. We fought for every mile.

Misha continued to lead. This was his third major Arctic expedition and he was very experienced at route-finding – which was just as well, because breaking trail was not simply a matter of moving on a given compass bearing. The magnetic field is very weak in high latitudes; Misha, Graeme and Gus would therefore simultaneously take bearings on a prominent lump of ice in the distance and Misha would make his way to it as best he could. The rest of us would follow.

Rupert had tried earlier on to explain to me the navigational problems peculiar to the area. North Magnetic Pole lies close to the north Canadian coast, in the Arctic Ocean, and for most of the way was behind us. The lines of magnetic variation are nearly parallel to the lines of longitude, changing as rapidly as one degree for every degree of longitude, and it is crucial therefore to know your longitude. That's the theory. In practice, in severe magnetic storms, fluctuations can put your compass setting out by as much as six degrees or more. We were marching through the worst magnetic storms and sunspot activity recorded for twenty years, and would have been in real trouble had we tried to navigate by compass alone, without daily confirmation of our position from the Argos satellite system. Receiving our position by radio each morning, Rupert plotted the co-ordinates on his map and determined the magnetic variation applicable to keep us pointing in the right direction. (See Appendix 1.) On those occasions when radio transmissions failed Rupert resorted to his sextant, but he found it very difficult to navigate by the sun and the moon.

A whole labyrinth of leads greeted us on Friday, 14th April. Nothing too complicated to begin with; the weather was clear, the air clean and hard. The wind lay still, and we were lulled into a false sense of ease. Then, during our third march of the day, a wind stirred from the east and dark clouds began to roll down from the north. We could feel the weather pressing in on all sides. Within minutes the sky was blocked out. We could not only sense danger, we could touch it. The atmospheric pressure seemed to have plummeted. Nervousness rippled through the group. We struggled into our windproof jackets as the wind gathered strength and visibility deteriorated rapidly.

During the early afternoon we marched into milk. The air was so thick with white I could not differentiate ice from sky. Somewhere behind or in front of me the sun shone weakly. Ghostly ridges of ice rose from the mist – the whole landscape had the feel of a deserted house, the furniture draped in sheets. The haze made me confused and clumsy as the path ahead dissolved into a featureless void. Only the compass told us we were heading north. We traversed vast fields of rough ice, feeling our way with our feet, falling and stumbling over sharp, unseen obstacles. We came across many small leads of open water and were forced to take off our skis to straddle them. The snow was soft and we sank deep, sometimes to our waists.

At around 8 p.m. we came across a jumble of pack ice heaped together like a great white refuse tip. We scaled to its jagged summit to be met with a disheartening sight. A field of thin ice stretched into the distance and a long stream of pressure ridges blocked the northern horizon. The grinding, aching sound of moving ice rang out of the mist towards us.

Misha climbed down from his vantage point to investigate the thin ice. It was less than a foot thick, about twenty centimetres, and we had to cross a hundred metres of it. We could see nothing to our right but a total white-out. To our left, no more than fifty paces away, the ocean pushed up savagely into the ice, driving through the dull whiteness like a freight train. The ice was forced up in front of our very eyes, moaning and gnashing. Huge plates were thrust vertically into the air and then went crashing down again into the dark ocean.

Huddled on the edge of chaos, we did not know which way to turn. The shore of ice opposite was coming straight for us – or we were travelling straight towards it. I had lost all sense of direction and perspective. The wind blew strongly in our faces; we could see nothing in the distance but the slow and sinister growth of fledgling pressure ridges.

We cowered in this place for twenty minutes, unsure if we should

90 A labyrinth of leads opens around the team
91 Encountering another jumble of pack-ice

press on. It was difficult to judge whether the ice was thick enough to support us. We listened and watched. The pushing and heaving of the ice pack seemed to come in waves and then as suddenly fell quiet. When Misha could see no further evidence of ice movement immediately in front of us he took several cautious steps on to the pack and we followed. We crossed the pressure ridges in our path without incident, moving quickly, the frightening chill of the place breathing down our necks.

Further on, conditions became so rough that there seemed no way out. The way ahead was strewn with great mounds and blocks, and in between the newer ice threatened to split beneath our tread, plummeting us straight into the ocean. Open water lapped nearby, and several times we trod on wet sludge. At that moment, in the gloomy light, the power of the ocean hit us with all its strength, its immensity, its cruelty.

Without skis we climbed on across the pressure ridges burrowing through the soft snow. My big sledge was a curse. I had called it back on the last resupply because I believed, as did the experts, that serious pressure ridge activity would have all but disappeared by now. In fact it was to be with us all the way to the Pole.

We fought on to the edge of a large ice field where all seemed quiet. There was no sign or sound of the predatory roving packs. Everyone was exhausted but we could find no safe place to pitch camp. It was my worst nightmare, a vision of the ice splitting beneath our tent as we slept, the eight of us tumbling into the blackness beneath, our cries muffled by our sleeping bags. So far there had been no need to post a night watch to guard against sudden shifts in the ice; Gus managed to do this in his sleep, waking to the slightest sound or disturbance.

So we moved on again, ducking and weaving through a maze of small open leads. Big, slow snowflakes landed softly on our faces. My kamiks were ruined and I shuffled along like a bagman. Eventually we stumbled across a large ice pan, seventy metres in diameter and surrounded by small translucent blue pressure ridges. Misha suggested we put the tent in the centre. Looking any further for somewhere safer this evening would be too risky.

Rupert and I battled with 'Dark Horse' but it wouldn't fire to life until the Headmaster had cleaned it. We drank tea before supper and quietly ruminated on the day. It was only later that Misha translated that night's diary entry for me. 'Situation seemed to me like in hell. I would not advise anyone to be in our situation. We climbed or crawled on over all these hindrances and I was afraid of injury. If somebody

92 The large sledges made crossing leads very difficult for Arved and Robert

broke his leg in that nightmare hardly could we get out. But endurance was compensated. At about 9 p.m. a clear perspective appeared. Instead of ice hills we came across ordered pressure ridge. I was aware of the fact we had a near escape from a dangerous place. The way ahead was easier.'

After supper Misha treated our many ailments. Arved's bleeding and frostbitten fingers were beginning to heal, Graeme's and Rupert's cracked hands seemed to be responding well to some unheard-of Soviet drugs. Not all his patients were doing so well. Darryl's heel was no better and Misha was reluctant to open the most recent blisters. The resultant pain, he guessed, might be too great for Darryl to bear.

He warned us not to drink too much water at this stage; he said it hindered the body's ability to adapt to the cold. The deep circles below Arved's eyes were not the result of tiredness or illness but the intake of too much fluid, Misha said.

In the mayhem of the following morning I was reminded again of my favourite North Pole account, Pooh Bear's: 'But if, every time I want to sit down for a little rest, I have to brush away half a dozen of Rabbit's smaller friends-and-relations first, then this isn't an Expo – whatever it is – at all, it's simply a Confused Noise.'

'I go now and not waiting for anybody,' Misha shouted.

'Oh, oh, this is serious,' I muttered to the others.

Everyone laughed but made haste. We could not afford to lose the Headmaster. Again the air was thick as porridge and visibility almost nil. Many times I stopped and shook my head, hoping that when I opened my eyes I would be able to see where the ice ended and the sky began. We fumbled along, feeling our way with our feet. We staggered and fell frequently. It was especially difficult for those encumbered with heavy packs to find their feet. As they thrashed and waved their ski poles about, trying to stand, they invariably just managed to bury themselves deeper.

After lunching quickly we ski'd on. The weather improved quite suddenly. The air cleared, the sun made a grand entrance from behind the clouds and the temperature rose dramatically. It was only around minus 20 degrees celsius and we could virtually travel in our underwear. There were more open leads, and a generous scattering of ice rubble, but we moved slowly in a long line without misadventure. We had had no radio contact with Columbia or Resolute for three or four days, no accurate confirmation of our position, and no way of knowing if the air drop scheduled for 17th April was to go ahead, whether we should seek a camp or press on with limited provisions. I worried, too, that these communication failures would not be helping the media's efforts to pull off the Ice Station deal.

Graeme made radio contact on the morning of the 16th and spoke briefly to Stephen at Columbia. The airdrop was scheduled to go ahead the following day but there was a danger that poor weather in Resolute could delay departure. The pilot had requested we make camp that afternoon and wait until he could locate us the following morning.

After breakfast Graeme and Gus set out first, Misha and I last. Misha soon caught up with those at the front while I assumed my now customary position at the rear with Darryl and Hiro. We followed Misha's tracks until we all re-assembled at the brink of a large expanse of open water. Graeme, Rupert and Darryl scouted to the west, Gus to the east. Misha slipped off his rucksack and set out on a lonely reconnoitre along the snow ridges which edged the lead. He soon found an easy and safe bridge across the open water and, taking a short cut back across the flat ice, suddenly popped back up in front of us.

'Follow that trail,' he said, pointing back the way he had just come.

We did as he said while he retrieved his pack. After we had disappeared behind the ridge, he took an even shorter route than before and suddenly appeared, a grinning apparition, in front of us once again.

We camped on a large flat plate of ice, near a recently formed lead of open water. Before going to bed Misha checked the site one last time. As he circled the tent he sank without warning through thin ice covering a small lead. The pack was obviously not as secure as it had appeared but it was too late now to move on. We had to take our chances that evening.

After supper we talked of home. Misha told us of his life in the Soviet Union, and we discussed expeditions past and future. That evening in our crowded tent, as I spoke of my South Pole journey, it dawned on me for the first time just how extraordinary that three-man odyssey had been. It had taken me three and a half years and a walk half way across the Arctic Ocean to realise the seriousness of that seventy-day march from Cape Evans to the Pole. I appreciated with the full force of hindsight what special men Roger Mear and Gareth Wood were, how grateful I was to them for guiding me South, how much they had taught me. I realised the value of their lessons not only technically but emotionally. The South had been a difficult learning ground; personality conflicts had so dominated our journey that now, on this much larger expedition, I was more content to take a back seat and lend emotional support and physical encouragement where necessary. Misha led, Graeme and Gus organised, and I trailed at the back picking up the pieces.

My back hurt terribly. Misha gave me some pain-killers and tried to ease the worst of the agony with massage. This particular injury had bothered me all my life but never more so than now. I had been told that the Arctic had a knack of prising the smallest problem wide open, of searching for your weaknesses and taking advantage of them. Misha said I had inflamed the injury by straining too hard against the harness in trying to negotiate my larger sledge through the contorted pressure ridges. The constant ache was beginning to fill every corner of my mind.

Everyone was more relaxed that evening. Misha went to bed with the sensation that 'we have lived through very complicated moment, now we have good crew, armed by perfect system. Even we have fewer quarrels, life puts everything in place.'

Misha was right: the team had found its stride at last. The 'machine' was almost in place, and we were moving quickly and safely across the worst and most dangerous ice we had seen. Now most of our arguments were amusing rather than divisive – Misha and Graeme

striding out in front, arguing furiously in pidgin English.

'Misha, we go this way,' Graeme would say.

'No, no, we go this way,' Misha would indicate in the opposite direction.

Arguments about the food, the hot chocolate, the stoves, the sleeping arrangements – the list went on but no problem was insurmountable. Only that one small rift which had come so early in the journey still lingered. While the evacuation of the slower team members had not been broached again, Darryl believed the attitude remained. 'You can cut it, it's so thick in the air,' he said to me.

Arved deplored this tear in the flag of team solidarity. 'Some people just want to get to the Pole and that is it, other people don't really know why they have come along in the first place. This lack of solidarity makes me feel sick.' His ideal was that everybody should, and must, get to the Pole because of the expedition's international character. If this small group of eight people was not able to work together and follow this ideal, how would nations be able to work together?

The tendency for bad feelings to emerge during and after any expedition is almost universal. Psychologists had warned me that this particular expedition provided 'a fair amount' of opportunity for becoming annoyed with each other. The fact that, on Icewalk, each team member was the sole representative of his country might make him feel more isolated rather than encourage overall unity. A culturally homogeneous group is safer, I was told. Cultural problems are not purely psychological but very closely related to survival.

With the exception of Hiro, I did not think Icewalk's cultural or language barriers had proved isolating. What isolation there was had been forged through differences in physical strength, capability and ambition. If there was one bond we had, among our many differences, it was our commitment to the expedition's aims and ideals. Of course we all wanted the Pole desperately, but it wasn't the substance of our endeavour; it was simply an exclamation mark.

Peary was sustained through defeat, incomparable hardships and the thinnest of hopes by that simple ambition of standing 'with 360 degrees of latitude beneath his motionless foot.'

We each had our own personal ambitions – Rupert and I would stand side by side at the Pole to become the first Britons to arrive on foot; Graeme the first Australian; Arved the first West German; Hiro the first Japanese; Darryl the first American and the youngest man

93 *Previous page*: Misha looks for a safe bridge to cross open water

ever; Misha the first Soviet from Canadian soil; Gus the first Inuit on foot, and myself first to walk to both Poles, North and South.

These ambitions were enough to sustain us through the most difficult times. But they were not enough to justify the expedition, and that realisation was all we had to unite us.

✳

On Monday, 17th April Rupert, Misha and I stood at the top of a long line of pressure ridges scanning the sky. We saw a small dot moving towards us from the south. The plane came in slowly and circled us several times but then banked to the south over our camp. Misha was concerned they were about to drop the entire payload on Darryl's and Hiro's heads as they worked inside the tent.

In fact they did not appear to be dropping anything; it seemed to be looking for a place to put down. We gathered our empty sacks and began to run towards the aircraft. The pilots had had some trouble locating us. On their first sortie they had spotted five people and had circled low, only to discover they were the Japanese Mako expedition, now some nine miles to our south.

We returned to the tent to read our mail and discuss the next phase of the journey. Plans for the floating ice station were proceeding; there were many 'ifs', but the Soviets were preparing to monitor our progress and measure this against the prevailing ice and tide movements nearer the Pole. They wanted an indication from us as to the likelihood of our

94   The resupply flight circles camp looking for a place to put down

arriving at the Pole by 10th May – or at the very latest by the 15th. Headquarters needed to know as soon as possible if we thought we had any hope of meeting this deadline. From the outset we had all been excited by the prospect of elevating Icewalk into an event which could have a real impact in the environmental sphere, and if this meant travelling almost twelve hours a day, as we were, eating and sleeping less, then we would do it. However, with temperatures now in the warm minus twenties and open leads of water multiplying daily, it seemed the Arctic Ocean itself was keen to sink us. We had heard news of vast tracks of open water nearer the Pole and sent word back to prepare the amphibious sledges, and to have an inflatable rubber raft on standby. Walk, row or swim, we would get there and we would meet the deadlines imposed. In some ways it was a relief to be forced to focus on an arrival date, to put this hellish exercise into some kind of perspective and feel that an end was in sight.

Little did we realise that back in the real world the project was already under threat. Television backers and the Soviet organisers were becoming nervous; ice conditions were less than favourable and our progress to date not encouraging. Christopher Holloway, who had ski'd the length of the Arctic Ocean with Misha on the Polar Bridge expedition, urged the director to err on the side of caution just as we were preparing to throw it to the winds. To meet the 10th May deadline, he warned, the team would have to abandon the slower members, abandon rest days, and therefore abandon the medical and scientific programmes.

As I considered the costs of a race I knew there was nothing that would persuade me to abandon Darryl – or anyone else – no matter what the price. 'You will march day and night but only six will stand at the Pole,' the clairvoyant Emma Drake had told me before we set out. I wondered now if she was right. She had, after all, predicted exactly when Roger, Gareth and I would arrive at the South Pole, just as she had predicted our financial salvation at Sir Jack Hayward's hands. For this expedition she had given me several pots of goose grease, excellent in the cold, and had delivered the disturbing prediction which plagued me now. Which two wouldn't make it?

No, I wouldn't let it happen. I could take some of Darryl's weight, and Hiro's if necessary, in my larger sledge.

The character of the expedition was changing; the continual rough ice, the endless pressure ridges, the flourishing maze of leads – all these things heightened our sense of urgency. Rupert's scientific programme, rather than Darryl's and Hiro's continued participation, was most immediately affected by this urgency. The cost of the programme had proved far greater than anyone had anticipated. The Arctic Ocean was a treacherous and unreliable laboratory. Taking your gloves off to collect snow samples posed the immediate risk of frostbite and the heavy scientific equipment had become a loathsome burden when every extra pound tugged cruelly at the harness. 'It was an ambitious programme,' Rupert said later:

> I realised almost immediately the expedition would not be a steady or leisurely journey. I had hoped to have a lot of time each day to complete my research, but the crippling temperatures of the first ten days made it a hell of a job. At first I froze three fingers, then I froze all of them and just as they were beginning to heal I froze another three, and so it went on. I had immense problems with the lids on the sample containers; they froze so hard it was almost impossible to get the tops off and with frozen fingers very painful to attempt to do so. The air pump, used for mercury sampling, was also very difficult to operate in the extreme cold.
>
> The sun phetometer was sent back on the first resupply: it was impossible to get the thing warm enough to use. I tried skiing with it inside my clothing but that didn't work. I suspended it from the tent ceiling in a plastic bag but this didn't work either.
>
> Our emphasis had changed by force of circumstance from a methodical scientific expedition to merely a race.

✳

Our position – 85 degrees 40 minutes North. Around 260 miles to go. Twenty-two days in which to do it. After decanting our resupply we took to the trail again at around 2 p.m. on Tuesday, 18th April. We enjoyed the extra heat and fuel – until we started hauling the packs and sledges made heavy by the additional provisions.

A light wind blew from the north and we donned our windproof jackets, to be met once again by dreadful ice conditions. The pressure ridges continued to mount one on top of the other; these incessant obstacles stretched in all directions and the snow in between was deep and grabbing. We often fell. Ahead of me, Hiro suddenly dropped from view and struggled in the snow for several minutes before rising to his feet. Each tumble seemed to exhaust him an unbearable degree further.

We entered a vast towering jungle of ice and zig-zagged our way through, often losing sight of each other, our heads low to the trail as we followed Misha's lead. We gathered after our fourth march in the early evening. Darryl was nowhere to be seen. We waited anxiously. He finally appeared from behind a large ridge of ice forty minutes later, solemnly holding a broken ski stick aloft. Fortunately for him, Hiro was carrying a spare.

We camped in a small area protected on all sides by large pressure ridges and set about our tasks quietly. Darryl spent time outside the tent seeing to his equipment; Arved made mugs of tea and a supper of buckwheat, pemmican, butter, oil and powdered milk, throwing the lot into one pot to simmer. All our mittens and socks were propped against the stoves or hung from the ceiling to dry. We unrolled our bags wherever we could find space; we had no 'sleeping system', as Misha called it, although Arved, Gus and Graeme liked to sleep as far from the tent's entrance as possible.

After supper Hiro fetched his journal while Graeme, Arved and I plugged in our Walkmans and tried to go somewhere else for a while. Fine Young Cannibals took me there. Misha disapproved of this pastime. He continually tried to speak to us, giving up finally and listening to music himself, but this produced in him an 'unnatural sensation of alien kind'. Misha believed the Arctic environment required our total application. The world outside our tent was hazardous and terrifyingly changeable. To survive one had to know it, and that meant total immersion in its every sound and movement. Misha worried about distractions of any kind – music or books. The few books which had set out with us had slowly disappeared. The last to go was Graeme's copy of *Sentinel* by James Michener. It, too, was ecologically recycled as lavatory paper.

After supper we pushed the stoves into the middle of the tent and Misha commenced surgery. My back was worsening rapidly, and I marched through much of the day with gritted teeth and the occasional involuntary tear. Misha rubbed a burning ointment into my lower spine, which seemed to offer some relief. I was very concerned. My back had never been this painful before. I was finding it difficult to bend at the waist and was forced to squat when picking something off the ground. Misha and the others had carried my weight that day, which helped, but I could not expect them to continue to do so.

The following morning Hiro complained of a sore throat, which turned out to be acute tonsillitis. Misha gave him some antibiotics and we prepared to move on. I refused to give over any of my weight this

95 Another cordon bleu supper
96 Hiro reads a letter from home

97 An uncrossable lead; the detour would cost many miles

day. Hiro travelled very slowly all morning, the sickness taking its toll. Graeme and Gus waited for him until Misha told Graeme to press ahead and break trail. Graeme looked surprised, but agreed, with pleasure. He had adapted to this place well and worked incredibly hard; Misha was pleased to see him flex his leadership muscles.

Hiro trailed far in the distance soon after setting out. Darryl walked back to help. When they finally joined us, we silently unpacked Hiro's things, leaving him with only his clothes and a sleeping bag and distributing the balance of his weight among everyone else – an additional five to six kilograms each.

Hiro travelled in the middle now and a little easier. In less than an hour we were drawn up short by a river of sea water thirty to forty metres wide. The river's banks were edged with paper-thin ice; the middle was just black water. We followed the tributary to our left for more than two hours in an attempt to find a place to cross. The river's banks were scarred with pressure ridges and travel was not easy. Graeme fell heavily in the deep snow, cursing loudly, waiting for us to pass before extricating himself and following on behind.

Misha suddenly noticed that the spare skis were missing. I felt

98 Crossing an open lead on a bridge of skis

dreadful because it had been my responsibility to carry them. Rupert and Gus, our most adept skiers, went back to look for them. We moved ahead, still looking for a crossing point. Gus and Rupert were gone for more than two hours, and in the meantime Misha found an area where the river narrowed and was bridged by ice which thinned dangerously for about two metres in the middle. He threw clumps of snow at this section to see if it would hold, then took off his skis, laid them atop the ice and gingerly crawled across the sagging bridge on hands and knees. Hiro followed, and we hurled our packs and sledges over the water to the two of them. I crawled across last, the cold water by this time welling up over the skis on to my gloves. Rupert and Gus rejoined us, having found the skis, and we set off hurriedly.

We were met immediately by another open lead of water. Misha sent Graeme west to search for a crossing while we moved east. The Australian soon called us in his direction. He had found a large plate of ice rising vertically out of the water which we were able to straddle. After we had crossed safely, a visibly tired Graeme asked Misha if we could take a break.

'We already lose enough time,' said Misha impatiently.

Graeme stood his ground. 'I'm not going to continue hauling fifteen pounds of Hiro's weight if that's the case,' he snapped. 'Let him do it.'

He slipped off his rucksack, fetched Hiro's and put it on the snow. Gus and Misha glanced at each other in bewilderment. Misha asked Graeme what he was doing.

'If Hiro can't carry his own weight and walk we should evacuate him,' Graeme announced.

We stood and watched in silence. Without a word, Arved picked up Hiro's pack and stowed it in his large sledge. I glanced at Hiro, wondering if he understood what had just happened.

Perhaps Graeme was exhausted. It had been a difficult day. Misha diplomatically tried to calm him. 'Graeme, Graeme – not many people on this expedition do job as well as you do. We need you.'

The rest of us said nothing.

That evening I suggested that Hiro go to bed as soon as we had the tent up. He slept through until breakfast. Misha massaged my back again, which helped ease the anguish temporarily.

Graeme made brief contact with Cape Columbia and learnt that we were only five miles from the 86th parallel. We also learnt that Pam Flowers had turned back – no reason was given. So now it was just the Mako expedition, the Soviets coming from the other side, and us.

Slowly I was settling into being here, adjusting to the wearing pace we must set. Many things kept me moving. I made a list in my diary to remind myself:

The cold
Getting to the Pole
My valiant friends
For the students who are this very evening departing Ottawa for
    Iqaluit and eventually Eureka
Because it's odd
Because we can do it
Because we can do something with it
Because nobody has ever done it
Because I'll never do it again

11

'ATTACK!'

After breakfast on 20th April Misha decided it was time to confront the challenge bluntly. He sat away from the warmth of the stove with his legs crossed and looked at each of us in turn, his eyes huge with seriousness.

'If we are going to reach Pole by 15th May we must work honestly and pull all our efforts,' he said. 'Those who will not do this must be deported back home.'

The Soviet doctor was using the same methods he had applied countless times before to stir the team to indignant action, to encourage us to dig deeper, even when to do so hurt us more than we imagined we could bear. I could not believe, however, that he really thought anyone should be returned to base – not after all we had been through. What he was doing was throwing down the gauntlet, quietly but firmly, in the genuine hope that it would be snatched up by each of us.

Misha had concentrated very hard on selecting the appropriate English words to convey his thoughts. Now almost five weeks into the journey, he had nothing but our unstinting respect, and despite his broken English we always understood exactly what he was saying. He treated the English language much as he treated the Arctic Ocean – with curiosity, respect and a determination to be the master.

I thought Misha's strategy had within it a great deal of wisdom. I almost always agreed with his decisions but now it was time for me, as company chairman, to give the managing director my total support, so that together we could ensure that this team got to the Pole intact. I endorsed his comments and everyone nodded, except Graeme. He thought that Misha should have said the same thing a fortnight ago.

We encountered more open water soon after setting out, although it did not appear as perilous as the leads which had riddled our path a day earlier. This sheet of water was fifteen metres wide and lapped at the base of some steep pressure ridges. Misha found a place where the

channel narrowed until it almost touched a small island of ice that was frozen to the opposite bank. The island's shores were too fragile to straddle with skis, but part of the channel was choked with snow and ice chunks. Misha threw a piece of ice on to this debris. It lodged, so Darryl, Arved and I began hurling lumps of snow into the channel until we had built a solid bridge. We inched across one at a time, knowing we were perched on a structure as precarious as a sandcastle, directly above the brooding ocean.

Forty-five minutes later we were on the move again.

'Good time', Misha said, 'for technically difficult crossing.'

Praise indeed.

The travelling became easier – until, that is, I smashed my ski pole. I fell to the back of the group, cursing under my laboured breath. Darryl had taken the last pole several days earlier. The appalling ice had chewed through all our spares. What was I going to do now?

It is virtually impossible to ski without a pole when hauling a large sledge. I wouldn't stand a chance in soft snow and it would require superhuman strength to coax my old sledge over the large ridges of ice. It was a dangerous situation. The loss of one small stick could leave me stranded, or slow the team to a point which jeopardised its chances of reaching the Pole.

I caught up with the others fifteen minutes after they had halted for lunch. We discussed ways of repairing the pole. What was needed was something to wedge inside the hollow staff to weld the two broken pieces together. We could think of nothing.

Then Misha said: 'Robert, you have that wood from Captain Scott's ship?'

Emma Drake had done it again. Before I left England, the clairvoyant had handed me a little bit of Scott's ship *Discovery*, to carry with me as a good luck charm. Had she foreseen its usefulness?

Rupert and I sent the others ahead. There was no point in their getting any colder than they already were. Misha did not like to split the group but eventually led them off towards the flat horizon.

Rupert filed down the piece of timber and I carefully chipped it into shape. If we made a mistake there would be no second chance. It was a delicate and difficult task in these temperatures, performed with a rough hacksaw and a pen knife. When we had finished we both paused. Nothing could have been more appropriate than for Captain

99 A convenient stepping stone
100 For Rupert, the expedition was the culmination of three years' work

Scott to help when no one else had been able to do so.

It was good to work with Rupert again and to talk of old times. In my determination to make Icewalk matter I had lost sight of a project that Rupert and I had envisaged three years earlier, and after which he still hankered – a simple four-man assault on the Pole. He would rather we had quietly, and without media fanfare, made our way to the top of the world, with the first evidence of our passing the publication of a book some twelve months later. Rupert was a traditionalist. He had fought hard and made sacrifices. During the first few weeks on the ice he had struggled silently, losing weight and scorching his fingers in the cold, straining to deal with an expedition which was proving much tougher than anyone had expected. But as the voyage unfolded Rupert seemed to emerge from his cocoon.

I enjoyed skiing side by side with him and listening to his tales of Arctic exploration. Rupert was our historical buff, and listening to him was as comforting as being tuned into Radio 4. He was so very British. I loved listening to his explanations of ionospheric disturbances and his accounts of famous and doomed expeditions, as much as I had the World Service in Antarctica. He had also become a rock in times of team crisis. From being one of Darryl's severest critics he had become one of the young American's staunchest supporters. Rupert wanted the team to win as a team, and he was one of the few to take time to explain discussions and decisions to Hiro when everyone else was simply too exhausted to break through the language barrier.

Rupert and I had shared many moments on the expedition but this was the most poignant. He held aloft the new ski pole and smiled. We had started this bloody thing together, his look said, and we were going to finish it together.

We followed the team's trail up pressure ridge and down ice pan, finally rolling into camp about an hour behind the others. We found them crouched in the tent, waiting for supper.

The team had carried Hiro's load again that day, and over supper he appeared to rally strength, becoming more animated than I remembered him since leaving Cape Columbia.

Misha called Hiro 'the silent one'. If questioned, he responded briefly, but rarely asked questions himself. During the day's rest breaks he usually sat apart from the remainder of the group, and in the evenings when we made camp he unpacked his things apart from the others. Misha once asked him why he sat alone. I don't want to hide the

101 Robert often chose to bring up the rear

102 Conditions rarely enable the team to march this closely together

sun from everybody, was the gist of Hiro's reply.

On this occasion, when we began discussing plans for the following day's travel, Hiro asked Misha to speak on his behalf because he did not understand what was being said. It was the first time he had entered into a team conversation voluntarily. Suddenly our silent friend began to speak. He said he thought the ice had been quite good today, but he still found the expedition very difficult. It was easier to be in the mountains, he said.

Hiro was not accustomed to hauling heavy weights, nor could he adjust to the constant grind of marching day in, day out, for hour upon endless hour. It was not as if Hiro was not a strong man. He was an accomplished mountaineer, his nine-year career including solo ascents of Huaskaran (6665m), Chopikarki (6400m), Pisco (6959m) in Peru, Chinborazo (6310m) in Ecuador and an unaccompanied winter ascent of Aconcagua (6959m) in Argentina. It was just that our form of expedition was totally alien to him and I don't think any amount of training could have prepared him for the physical and mental stamina required for Polar exploration. The mountain is taken in short

concentrated bursts. The Pole is a war of attrition.

While accustomed to isolation, Hiro was also very gregarious – always the first to lead the charge to one or two very questionable bars in Iqaluit, always the first to smile. He was an uncanny mimic and, in his first week of joining the team in Iqaluit, mastered many suspect elements of Australian and American colloquial vocabularies, in addition to Gus's very distinctive laugh. Yet, despite Hiro's quick grasp of essential English phrases, he shared little with us. I wondered if he mourned the recent loss of his friends on the side of a Canadian mountain, whether he missed home, whether this journey was destroying him. During the day I loaned him my red jacket because he was usually cold. Misha also offered his.

Misha was pleased to hear Hiro speak that evening. The Soviet invested the best part of his time in getting to know and understand his companions, but Hiro had proved a persistent enigma. Misha's insatiable curiosity about all things, his kindness, patience and tireless energy overwhelmed us at times. When everyone else was too tired, or cold, to be bothered about much, Misha attended surgery – morning and evening, without fail – administering to our mental as well as our physical fatigues.

On 21st April the list of ailments included deep painful cracks in the skin of Rupert's dry hands, a bad rash on Graeme's back, my damaged spine, which the doctor massaged again, and Darryl's foot. The blistered heel had begun to open, risking infection. The wound was red raw and seemed to be deepening. Misha and I would not allow Darryl to look at the ulceration, which could prove his nemesis.

*

Next morning the new regime struck; up at 5.30 a.m. in readiness for an all-out day. Graeme managed to make radio contact, but we received disturbing news. A party which had just flown to the Pole reported continuous rough ice to 87 degrees North, and beyond this point countless leads and stretches of open water – some many miles wide and long. About forty miles from the Pole the ice piled up again.

So now we knew.

The day which followed was kind, and we were presented with many great pans of flat ice. In fact it was probably the easiest skiing we had enjoyed since 20th March, and for the first time we managed nine sixty-minute marches: 540 minutes of travelling time.

'Equivalent to eleven fifty-minute marches!' Misha cried triumphantly. 'This is splendid result. I remember never such a long working day on any expedition.'

That night we were tired but elated. Hiro and Darryl were particularly weary, Hiro most of all. It has been a hard day, he told me, we walked too far. He tried to explain to Misha how unaccustomed he was to this continual drudge. Hiro was struggling hard and, despite his determination and mine, I wondered if he really would make it. I would not rule out the possibility of his evacuation to Eureka, but that would be his decision and nobody else's – as it had been Darryl's to come with us on 20th March.

Before setting out the next day Graeme received word of our position from Jeremy in Resolute – 86 degrees 20 minutes North. So we had covered fifteen nautical miles the previous day, a record. What cheered me more, however, was the news that our students had arrived at Eureka. If conditions held, we should soon be in radio contact with them.

Over breakfast someone suggested bringing our next resupply forward a day to the 25th. Misha would not hear of it.

'We have rations to last only to midday of the 26th,' Arved warned.

Misha insisted we push on. We could well afford to risk a little hunger, he said.

Graeme disagreed. 'I have no intention of marching without food. If the weather was to turn and the flight delayed by several days we would have taken a needless risk.'

Misha dug in his heels: 'The main task is to go on and on. Though we take care, we generally in good shape. There is nothing dangerous in having no food for the evening of the 26th. In any case, we can spend day or two on small rations to guard against eventuality. Principal position, and major concern, is fuel, and we have enough of that.'

He argued that each resupply wasted at least two days and while conditions were so favourable it would be insane not to press on as quickly as possible. We had risked hunger before and could do it again.

'I will not march without food,' Graeme said. 'If you delay the resupply I am going to fly back out with it.'

'If you bring resupply forward I quickly fly back with it,' Misha countered.

'International co-operation,' I muttered, loudly enough to interrupt their dispute.

Rupert and I did our best to act as intermediaries, but arguments between Graeme and Misha did tend to become quite protracted. This one was cut short as we emerged from the tent and the wind blew their angry words into the snow.

103 Graeme snatches ten minutes of precious sleep

104 Sometimes it was better to file between the leads than to confront them

We distributed Hiro's load between us again, hoping he would soon gather strength for the three long weeks which still stretched before us.

The ice was less brutish today. We crossed many low rows of pressure ridges and rough ice, skirting small ponds of open water. During the afternoon, while we paused for a brief rest, collapsed on our packs and sledges on a small floe, we were able to watch the ice gently ridging all around us, less than three metres from where we sat. It sighed and groaned, rising slowly into the air. 'I feel I am sitting in theatre for very special performance,' Misha said.

During the afternoon we filed between the leads rather than confronting them. I was happier on the flat ice, pressing into the traces as I listened to the soft whoosh of the sledge runners behind me. I felt I could breathe again.

We made camp behind the shelter of a small pressure ridge as the wind seemed to be building. That evening the radio crackled to life with ease. Hiro was able to speak to the *Yomiuri* photographer based in Eureka. It was wonderful to see him so animated and obviously relieved at being able to speak in his own language again. Misha tried to speak to Kirill, the Soviet student escort and former Polar Bridge radio operator. He tripped and stumbled over his words, having difficulty coming to terms with his mother tongue again after concentrating so intently on mastering English.

Resolute signed off with a coded message: Would Darryl be coming out?

'Negative,' Graeme replied.

Base confirmed that the students were to touch down at Eureka later that evening. I tried to visualise their arrival. They would be confused by the perpetual daylight. At 2 a.m., when they disembarked, the sun would not have laid down its head, the evening light would simply have shifted a little. I closed my eyes and could see the 748 winging its way across the mountains, streaming cold from the lowered undercarriage. The Arctic hares would gaze up lazily and then lope away across the frozen tundra. I hoped the wolves would be there watching as the youngsters emerged from their capsule of warmth to smack into a rock-solid wall of cold.

The following morning radio communications held. We had travelled about thirteen miles the previous day and camped at 86 degrees 33 minutes North. The ice was complicated again. Darryl and Hiro appeared stronger but Misha and I still worried about Hiro's ability to make the distance. Graeme and Gus complained several times about the burden of his extra weight.

During the afternoon we were skiing across a large field of ice covered in drifting snow. Out front Misha amused himself by recognising shapes in the soft, undisturbed surface – a person, a house, a footprint. Another footprint. And another. And the unmistakable tracks of a snowmobile. We had found the Mako expedition.

The prints were fresh, snow had not drifted to fill them in, despite the strong wind. We stood and discussed our find; the prints appeared to be heading east so we did not follow them. On their large and noisy machines they were forced to skirt many of the obstacles we could simply climb, straddle or leap.

Later we came across the Mako tracks again, together with some fuel stains and a cigarette butt. We climbed to the top of a tall ridge but could see no sign of the expedition, which must now be very near. We followed their tracks for some time and found where they had hacked their way through a large pressure ridge, using ice picks and axes, to make a path for their machines. It seemed an unnecessarily violent intrusion into this silent, beautiful wilderness.

That evening we made our first contact with the students. While we could not see them we could picture the scene – the Polar Haven

105 Stephen Williams helps members of the student expedition make contact with the Polar team

crammed with students, television and film crews, journalists and photographers all glowing a strange orange as the light filtered through the thin walls of the tent. The radio would be crackling in the corner. Eventually Graeme's faint and static-ridden voice would be detected. They would listen patiently to our shopping list – a replacement radio, a complete change of clothing for Hiro, new sleeping bags for Hiro and Arved, Misha's reserve medical box, Graeme's kilo of peppered salami, Misha's kilo of raw bacon.

When the shopping was over, Tessa from New Zealand spoke to us. She was so nervous and so far away we could barely hear her. Graeme sat crouched over the radio adjusting various dials but before we could speak to anyone else the signal began to break up and we lost them. I could not believe they were actually there and speaking to us. I felt very proud. This moment concluded a fine day in all respects. In one day we had seen everything. The weather was sunny in the morning, then it clouded over, it was still and then the wind blew, it was fresh, then it became cold, we encountered rough ice, then perfectly flat ice, then open leads and then great sheets of open water covered in treacherously thin ice, then thick ice, then pressure ridges, then deep snow. We had rushed along perfect ice fields and then fallen laughing into deep snow drifts. We had passed beneath clear skies and dark heavy clouds suspended above still black waters. And through it all we had walked ten one-hour marches, 600 minutes.

'Three weeks ago, I would not believe, for love of money,' Misha laughed.

I was just as astonished when I remembered those first two weeks of our journey, when five fifty-minute marches had taken all day and almost destroyed us. Now we were at 86 degrees 49 minutes North, and had just travelled sixteen miles, a new journey record on a day which had tested every skill we had acquired in the last few weeks.

Greatly encouraged as we were, we sat in the tent and confronted, for the first time, the tensions and hardships which looked set to become worse as the days and the Pole slipped further away from us. We spoke of the possibility of the weaker having to return to Eureka. I did not believe this was really an option, but I thought that perhaps its airing would convince everyone of the seriousness of the task ahead.

All the while Misha attended to surgery. Darryl's foot was beginning to deteriorate badly, despite the doctor's constant attention. It was difficult to undo, each evening, the damage wrought during ten hours of travel across the ice during the day. I watched Misha patiently bandaging the wound after photographing the lesion, and realised then that if we were ever to get to the Pole as a team it would be due almost entirely to the knowledge, energy and kindness of this man. And yet I had never expressed my appreciation.

Misha and I were the last to leave the tent the next morning. I put a hand on his shoulder and said: 'I thank you, Misha, very much, for all you are doing for us.'

The Russian looked at me with surprise. He had been about to put on his rucksack; now, visibly moved, he embraced me and said how happy he was to have met me and for us to have worked together. We agreed that nobody had to be sent back from Icewalk, that these talks were needed only for stimulation. The important thing now was to keep morale high.

At that moment I recognised how close I had become to Misha and how heavily I relied upon his experience and judgment – in spite of the aggravation we often caused each other. Misha was clearly touched by the utterance of a simple 'thank you' and sped to the front of the group wearing a wide smile before roving the line in his strong, paternal manner.

Gus was in a dark mood that day. I think he was still homesick. He missed his wife, who was heavy with their first child, and he just wanted the thing over with.

I liked Gus a lot and I understood his frustration. He was a hard man and very self-contained. As a child he had been taken from his natural Inuit family in Inuvik (the Mackenzie Delta) as part of a Canadian Government integration programme involving thousands of Inuit children. He was raised by a Western family and educated in a Western school. He saw his natural parents for only two months of every year. Half of his life had been spent in the South and he had adjusted well to that style of living.

'My yearning for the Arctic was never there until last year when I returned to the North to take up a position as a conservation education officer with the Canadian Department of Renewable Resources,' he had said to me before the expedition began. 'I got to know the people a lot more, got to know their concerns for the environment and how important it is for their lifestyle and their ability to maintain some form of cultural identity. I knew Icewalk could put me back in touch with my environment, giving me a greater appreciation of my parents and ancestors, who endured all their lives what I would have to endure for only a few weeks.'

There was no doubt that Gus was at home in this environment. He simply took in his stride the cold, the food, the travel. Yet here he was, longing to have it over with and to return home.

Gus moved at the head of the pack as we pushed on, hoping for another big day. We encountered a long lead of water covered with a wafer-thin layer of ice. Misha asked Hiro to fetch a rope. Taking one end, he edged his way painfully slowly across this brittle skin to the opposite side of the lead. The ice held firm and we crossed cautiously, holding the rope that was suspended between Misha and Hiro.

The weather began to turn, heavy clouds scudding across the sky. The ice was rough and the drift strong; at times we watched the water flow a few centimetres beneath our feet. Floes moved with a wave-like motion as we travelled over them. We crossed more open water and tackled more rough ice before climbing a very high range of pressure ridges whose northerly face dropped away steeply. The sharp descent posed a problem for most of us. Arved's personal solution involved him dangling on the top of the ridge, his sledge one side and he the other. As for me, I pushed my monster over the top and went crashing down head first. Thankfully the snow was soft.

Towards the end of the last march we encountered more rough ice. Uncharacteristically, Misha suggested that we halt prematurely and

106 Despite Robert's expectations, conditions rarely favoured the larger sledges
107 Tiredness was compounded by frequent falls

109 Dark skies meant the threat of open water was never far away

make camp.

'No way,' I said. 'Attack!'

Misha agreed reluctantly. He could see I was determined to see out the marching day.

We made brief contact with Columbia and learnt, much to Misha's relief and Graeme's chagrin, that the resupply would be with us on the 26th.

Hiro's eyes had been damaged by the sun. He sat in the tent that evening keeping them firmly shut, except occasionally to allow Misha to plop in some more drops.

The weather was definitely warmer that evening. I decided to sleep outside and made myself a bed in my sledge.

108 *Previous page*: Cautiously crossing a frozen lead, roped for safety

12

FACES IN THE ICE

'One hundred and eighty!' I cried, emulating the darts referee at the top of my voice. I had been waiting for this moment since the expedition began.

One hundred and eighty miles to go . . . My excitement on arriving at the 87th parallel was not understood by the others, but they shared my relief at notching up another sixty miles, ticking off another parallel. 87, 88, 89 and then the Pole. We were more than half way across this infernal ocean, and for the first time I began to sense an end to the journey.

Camped at exactly 87 degrees North, sitting in a tiny tent in the middle of nowhere, I wondered if this was really happening, if I was really walking to the North Pole. I thought of people doing normal things – driving, sleeping in a bed, shopping, eating dinner at a table. These things suddenly seemed incomprehensible; the whole world seemed a blur. I was overwhelmed by a feeling of dislocation, the same sense of panic as waking in the dark in a strange place, eyes wide open, yet not knowing where you are.

The perpetual daylight played tricks with the mind. It is difficult to know, until one is deprived of one or the other, how deeply our existences are dictated by light and darkness. With the sun never setting, simply circling our shrinking horizon, time had no bounds. It was measured in sixty-minute struggles, fifteen-minute breaks, sixty-minute struggles. The light gave one, too, a false sense of immortality, of not needing to sleep. Nothing but exhaustion could drive us to our sleeping bags, and exhaustion now took up the attack reluctantly relinquished by the cold.

Exhaustion was followed by vagueness. Misha spent an entire day looking for his balaclava while I ferreted around for a spoon I had lost. Graeme eventually spotted the balaclava on Misha's head and after a day's uncomfortable travel I found the spoon in my boot.

We stepped off the 87th parallel on Tuesday 25th April. I stole a cigarette before breakfast while the Headmaster wasn't looking, and after rolling up my sleeping bag repacked my sledge. I realised that my sledge had become a sort of living thing full of odds and ends – post-cards, scraps of paper with scrawled thoughts for future projects, pots of Royal Jelly and Ginseng tablets, my frostbite preventative. Darryl hobbled over, peered at my collection of bric-a-brac, and laughed.

'Robert, you just don't fit out here, do you?' he said, pointing to the red bandana wrapped around my balaclava. 'You don't look like an Arctic explorer, yet here you are, one of the world's leading experts on epic walks, and you hate walking.'

Darryl and I often laughed at the absurdity of voluntarily hauling to the North Pole. We travelled together at the rear, him shuffling along trying to push the pain to the back of his mind, his face vacant, me talking continually: 'Darryl, if the Martians were circling earth now looking for its craziest inhabitants, when they saw us at 87 degrees North chewing on raw bacon and trying to burn the tent down they wouldn't look any further.'

I wanted to remind him we were still human creatures and not mindless survival machines. When we sat in the tent in the evening, eight men adrift on the ice screaming at each other about the stoves, I would catch Darryl's eye and he would burst into laughter its infectiousness immediately defusing the tension.

110 Breaking trail

I tried to show Darryl that you don't have to be an explorer to explore.

'When I was a child I could not navigate my way out of the local wood without the help of my sister Lucinda,' I teased. 'I've never been an explorer. I walked to the South Pole because it gave me something to talk about to girls at parties.'

Wally Herbert once said: 'And of what value is this journey? It is well for those who ask such a question that there are others who feel the answer and never need to ask.'

Yet I asked myself this question every day. I don't belong to the clique of world explorers. To be frank, exploration is not that difficult; latter day explorers and their attendant publicity machines have on the whole perpetuated a myth. There is no denying it is hard and dangerous work, but it's a lot tougher to turn up to a factory at 5 a.m. six days a week or to sit behind a desk for two thirds of your life.

Exploration is a tremendous liberty and privilege. The simplicity of existence, alone on the ice, frees the soul. From this place, as I am sure it is possible from the summit of a mountain peak, one can see things more clearly. Isolation is a source of great strength and release.

✳

It was Arved's birthday on 26th April, but the gods were not smiling on him. Despite perfect weather – visibility of twenty kilometres with good contrast and only a slight breeze – still we could not locate a suitable landing strip for the resupply flight.

Graeme spoke briefly to Crispin at Cape Columbia, although the signal was weak and unreliable. An uncharacteristically agitated Crispin told us to find a strip immediately: the plane was on its way. After hauling some four miles more we eventually stumbled across a long, wide and flat frozen lead of water, but we had no time to prepare it before the aircraft arrived. In any case, we were exhausted. Having discarded food so we could travel lighter and faster, we had been existing on half rations.

The Twin Otter glided to a smooth halt; the strip was good and held firm. Hiro disappeared to the tent with a new set of clothing that had been dispatched to boost his shattered morale. I couldn't bring myself to return my damaged ski pole, the little piece of *Discovery* still firmly wedged within it. I kept it with me for luck.

There was mail for all of us. I opened one of my letters to discover that the Soviet Ice Station project had fallen through. It was beyond belief. We had been marching ten to twelve hours a day with sick

111 and 112 Robert receives confirmation that the Soviet Ice Station project has
fallen through, and makes his feelings known to base camp

and injured men until our bodies and brains were numb. Rupert had
all but abandoned his scientific programme, and we were punching
for the Pole to meet a deadline imposed suddenly upon us two weeks
earlier. Now, just as suddenly, that deadline had been taken away.

Brought up short in its tracks, the team paused on Thursday for a
collective breath. I paced impatiently all day as we drifted north three
more precious minutes and Misha sat bent over his centrifuge sorting
the blood he had extracted from us. On Friday, too, we remained in
camp. Graeme connected the new banks of batteries to the radio and
prepared for an almost full day of transmissions to the students in
Eureka.

I tried to discover what had happened to the Ice Station project,
shouting through a cloud of static across the frozen miles. A
complicated four-way conversation ensued between myself and Stephen
in Eureka, Jeremy in Resolute and the film director in London. The Ice
Station project was off but there was a chance of transmitting from a
fixed Soviet ice station 1,000 kilometres from the Pole. I was not wild
about the idea, and Misha asked Kirill, the Soviet student escort, to
make contact with the Soviets direct. He did, but they could not

confirm that the alternative project would go ahead, although they had dispatched a small team to the fixed Ice Station to begin necessary preparations. Misha and I were determined to resolve the problem. I refused to be dangled on a string, in this of all places.

A more detailed message was then relayed to me from Ottawa. Apparently plans for Ice Station North Pole had had to be abandoned because of uncertainty over the date of our arrival and safety concerns as a result of early break-up of ice this year. The closer we now were to the original target of 16th or 17th May the better. Alternative plans included a live satellite press conference out of Resolute.

We had been told all along that 15th May would be soon enough to arrive, but what could I do about the situation? We were trying to serve two masters diametrically opposed: this temperamental environment and the foibles of the media. All we could do was to march north and await further developments.

Misha commandeered the radio to contact Kirill. They spoke slowly and seriously in Russian for some time. Kirill pestered Stephen to allow him to contact the Soviet Union, and information filtered back to us in dribs and drabs as we continued the push north. We heard a different story from the Soviet side. They believed the cancellation was due to lack of finance; they had already announced on Soviet television that there would be a satellite link with the North Pole. All technical equipment had been flown to the Soviet station MP31.

I told Resolute that we were pressing for the North Pole at the earliest possible date of 10th May. We simply could not spend any longer on the ice, and now we had favourable conditions it would be mad to slow our progress, otherwise we might encounter ice break-up ourselves.

'Sorry,' I shouted to beat the static, 'but the race was started at *your* end. Tomorrow, 1st May, we hope to be at 88 degrees North. We have just covered two degrees of latitude, 120 nautical miles in nine days, therefore 10th to 12th May is a more realistic date. If the ice station plan fails we will have to accept whatever comes in its place. We are going for it. We cannot stop.'

If nothing else we had to beat the break-up of the ice. The amphibious sledges and raft were on standby and could well be needed. The temperature hovered at around minus 15 degrees celsius; the sun, whose warmth could now almost be tasted, circled our small world, casually prising apart the ice as it passed.

We decided to begin marching through the night when the temperature was at least five degrees colder and the leads of water,

113 A welcome stretch of flat ice

which now flourished about us, were more likely to be frozen. Great tracts of pressure ridges still barred our passage north but they were not as severe a problem as the open water which we could see in the distance, reflected darkly in the sky. Water sky they called it: sky, ice, water, a treacherous collage.

On Friday night we travelled ten nautical miles. On Saturday we slept. In the evening we battled for a mammoth thirteen and a half hours, covering sixteen miles, equal to our best day's travel. Conditions had thankfully remained clear and the contrast good. The temperature had dropped to minus 21 degrees and I prayed for it to become colder. The pack was beginning to bounce like sponge beneath our feet. We could hear the ice crack, the sounds cannoning towards us. Everything told us we should keep moving but I was worried about how long we could sustain the pace. It was killing Hiro and Darryl. How would we know when we had pushed them too far?

On Sunday night we managed another fourteen nautical miles and made camp in the morning at 88 degrees North. I found the tent too hot and crowded and slept outside, tucked deep in my sleeping bag, listening to the ocean's ceaseless moan.

At breakfast I sat in silence. I was so tired that even talking seemed to consume too much energy. I gazed at the faces around me. They had changed again. Darryl's black skin was flecked with the white scars of frostbite, Rupert's cheeks were swollen and his eyes puffy. Hiro's eyes were glazed, he was so exhausted he was barely with us any more. Arved's nose was mottled with frostbite and he seemed shrivelled; even Graeme and Gus had that look of shell-shocked tautness about their faces.

Exhaustion is self perpetuating. I found it exhausting to be exhausted. Anyone who has put in an eight-hour day cross-country skiing knows weariness; stretch this out to thirteen hours a day carrying or hauling 150 pounds, constantly negotiating walls of ice, streams of freezing water and deep soft snow and then imagine this day after day after day.

A chair would have been nice at that moment. My back was grinding me down; it was the harness and the crouched tent life. The pain came in waves.

On Monday night, as we ski'd wearily out again following Misha's lead, I noticed a Pan Am Jumbo flying overhead. I looked up from the frozen waste, shielding the sun from my eyes, and thought of the hundreds of people asleep in those amazingly comfortable chairs. My eyes savoured the blue of the stewardesses' uniforms, the rainbow of passengers' clothes. I imagined the luxury of awakening in the warmth, of pressing a button and having a fabulous woman lean over me. In my mind I ordered five meals and five bottles of champagne. I tried to remember what it was like to smell things: the scent of this woman's perfume would be staggering and probably make me pass out.

The hours passed, some quickly, some slowly. The team moved almost as one. Each man had a grim, hunched look of determination about him as if his body were frozen but for the mechanical movement of arms and legs. By Tuesday we had travelled a further twelve nautical miles. The weather had turned, visibility was reduced to less than one-and-a-half miles. Contrast was almost non-existent. Wearily

114 Crawling like insects across the thinner ice, with skis laid out like a raft

we ploughed on, heads down, not letting the conditions deter us, often stumbling over imagined obstacles as we followed Misha's unfaltering trail.

The Mako expedition had crossed the 89th parallel to be greeted with a delta of open leads. Their resupply flight had been delayed as they travelled west looking for a place for the aircraft to put down: satellite photographs showed low cloud and misting, indicating even more open water, well beyond 89 degrees. The last miles were not to be easily won.

By Thursday morning only another thirty miles lay between our camp and the 89th parallel. The ice was flat; many of the leads were short and we were usually able to skirt them. Sometimes we had to crawl like insects across the thinner ice, our skis laid out like a raft. The temperature had rocketed to minus 10 degrees and skiing was now a sweating toil.

Darryl had become almost intoxicated by pain. The blisters on his heel had burst long ago and the raw skin gradually peeled and chafed away as it rubbed against his boot. The horrifying wound had worn to the bone. Misha treated the festering sore as best he could, making sure that Darryl never saw his injury during the few minutes it was unbandaged each day. We were convinced that if he did, he would be demoralised beyond hope. Pain helped him to focus on every step; pain made every minute of the journey matter. But how far could he travel before the pain became unbearable, the risk of serious damage to the bone untenable?

I ski'd by his side for much of each day, carrying some of his weight and conjuring distractions for his heated brain.

'Let's play a game,' I suggested that Thursday. 'Let's try and guess what animal each of our friends is, starting with Rupert.'

'A fox', Darryl said after some thought, 'an Arctic fox.'

'Graeme's a sort of bird,' I said. 'Flying around, so busy he's a blur.'

'A kingfisher,' said Darryl.

We both agreed Gus was a cat – jumpy and finicky but always immaculately groomed.

'And Arved's a dog,' I mused.

'A Saint Bernard,' Darryl elaborated, 'large and shaggy; quiet but strong.'

I saw Hiro as an Emperor Penguin. Darryl considered him a panda, playful and always eating at the outset of the journey but later withdrawing into himself and becoming sleepy as if hibernating.

I suspected Darryl could be a young eagle constantly tumbling from

115 Robert hauls his load across a narrow lead. The man behind carries his on
his back.

his nest, or a young thoroughbred horse, strong but undisciplined.

Darryl thought I was a dolphin – 'Strong, adaptable, communal but independent; ever the optimist.'

Misha was a panther, on that we both agreed – a black panther, all stealth and strength. Nothing paralleled his ability to deal with the environment, the people or their problems. He could lead us for twelve hours across broken ice in poor contrast, then repair the stoves, cook, treat our injuries for an hour and speak quietly into his dictaphone while we slept.

Radio communications had dropped away again. We heard little from the outside world other than that the North Pole Ice Station project had definitely been scrapped. I no longer cared, I was beyond disappointment. We were locked into the race regardless. This place was giving no quarter and would most certainly beat us if we did not hurry.

We began to cheat time by marching fourteen hours a day. A further six were eaten up sorting the camp morning and evening, leaving only four in which to sleep. We desperately needed more rest; Misha's solution was to invent the 26-hour day.

On Saturday, 6th May, we sat at 88 degrees 54 minutes North, sixty-six miles from the Pole. On the same day the Soviets arrived at the top of the world, tragically with the loss of one man and the evacuation of another. It was a courageous effort. We had hoped to meet them at the Pole but that no longer seemed a possibility.

We set out again on Saturday afternoon, travelling until 4 a.m. Sunday morning. The weather was closing in all the time. The radio had gone down; we had less than one day's food and fuel remaining. A resupply had been scheduled for that day but there was no chance of it landing in these conditions. We could not radio base to warn them, so we did the only thing we could: we transmitted a coded message via Toulouse using the Argos beacon – 'Weather unsuitable for resupply'. We hoped the message got through.

After making camp I collapsed into my sleeping bag away from the tent and the noise, not bothering with supper. It was sleep my body needed, not food. Rupert brought me hot chocolate. I traded him my biscuits.

I slept fitfully that night and dreamt of the bodies of Scott and his companions. It was a dream I had often. I saw the ice moving them slowly closer to the edge of the Antarctic continent, where one day they would sail off in an iceberg like Vikings toward the sun, towards home.

13

THE FINAL DASH

On Sunday, 7th May, we learned that we had travelled five miles beyond the 89th parallel. We were pleased, but the feeling did not hold us for long. All thoughts were tuned to our final resupply which had been jeopardised by the threat of a blizzard.

Our aircraft had departed Resolute for Eureka on the Friday evening, hoping to be able to take advantage of any small break in the weather. By Saturday evening the weather had not improved. The resupply was postponed until Sunday, but Sunday arrived and the clouds still hung low to the horizon. The weather was grim, blowing snow; visibility was poor. We knew the pilot could not land in such conditions.

We were in a tight position. The weather showed no sign of lifting, our food and fuel were almost gone, yet we had to push on, marching up to eighteen hours a day.

After snatching a few hours' sleep on Sunday morning Graeme got back to work on the radio. He eventually broke through, but only for a few brief minutes. Plans for a full resupply were to be abandoned, he told base. He requested an urgent airdrop of essentials. There was no way now that we could move on until they arrived. We huddled in the tent and waited.

The aircraft departed Eureka at midnight on Sunday and refuelled at Bradley's floating fuel cache, located mid-way to the Pole. At 5 a.m. on Monday morning we heard the sound of the aircraft as it ploughed through the thick cloud. There was no hope of landing. Clouds blocked out the sun, giving the pilot no means of judging the ice beneath him. The plane made several low passes before the rear door was flung open. Jeremy, strapped in with a length of rope, began hurling our provisions on to the ice. The first drop landed only a hundred metres from camp. The Twin Otter made several more passes, skimming as low as three metres from the ice. The skill and daring of these Arctic pilots never failed to confound me.

We rushed round gathering up our supplies as the aircraft rose sharply, banked away into the clouds and was swallowed. There were no rafts, no amphibious sledges, no magic black box to help us accurately locate the Pole. They would have shattered on impact with the ground. Most of the boxes of provisions had withstood the drop, but for sixteen litres of orange juice that lay splattered over a snow drift: perhaps the largest orange sorbet ever prepared.

We returned to the tent and began to unpack our supplies. Misha prepared to draw more blood. News arrived from headquarters confirming that we were to be met by the world's press in Resolute, where the town's tiny satellite station was currently being reactivated. It meant arriving at the Pole no later than the morning of 14th May.

With new batteries we managed to get through to Eureka and I was able to deliver a final – and for me, sad – message to the students before they departed the Arctic for home. 'We have tried our best as a team to see you,' I said. 'But for safety reasons, and the dictates of the media, we are not making a final push until 14th May. We have tried our hardest, we are now in position for the Pole. We wish you all the very best.'

We sat around the belching Soviet stoves and discussed the revised

116 Rupert takes a sighting with the artificial horizon

press conference plan. It was worrying; the schedule was too tight. It could take us more than twelve hours to pinpoint the Pole accurately once we were in its general vicinity, and the weather posed a very real threat to the turn-around evacuation required by the press conference organisers. We could only hope that our luck would hold.

We remained camped on Monday to allow Misha to complete his medical tests, and took the opportunity to draw breath for the final dash. As we sat we drifted four miles south.

We did not set off again until Tuesday. On the advice of our resupply pilot we pushed north east to pass between two large open leads of water which he had spotted from the air. The path ahead was rumoured to be riddled with leads, and many of them appeared uncrossable.

The days and nights which followed blurred into each other. Marching and sleeping encroached upon each other, then became one and the same. Men slept on their packs during each fifteen-minute break. We seemed to haul around the clock, pushing beyond the bounds of exhaustion to some strange state of being where thoughts lay scattered all over the place. The past rushed forwards to confuse itself with the present; friends and family and long-forgotten memories hovered before my eyes.

I ski'd in a daze, squinting at the ice that stretched brilliantly in all directions. The weather was so warm – minus 2 degrees celsius – that I saw the horizon swill like soup, stirring ice through cloud. I became disorientated, had to navigate through cloud after rolling cloud of weariness by staring at the tips of my skis and following them. I looked up sometimes to be greeted by dark pools of water; a black reminder that we were four hundred miles from land.

Misha forged out beneath the warm spring sun, route-finding in a place which was cracking and opening up about us. He weaved in all directions to avoid the open water. We followed with our eyes glued to his ski tracks. Many times Misha was forced to double back on the opposite side of an open lead. At the end of the team and at least twenty minutes behind him, occasionally I would glance up and see him standing only yards away from me across a sheet of open water. We would wave and continue on our way silently.

Poor contrast and thick cloud marred our last few days. Graeme and Gus helped Misha break trail. We often ski'd blind in a gentle blizzard colliding with pressure ridges or disappearing suddenly into a pillow of deep snow. We were all falling heavily and falling often; the risk of injury had never been greater and I urged everyone to take care.

Hiro was oblivious to everything but the two ski tracks beneath his glazed stare. At one point Darryl fell heavily into deep snow, almost burying himself. Hiro ski'd straight over Darryl without noticing him at all. Darryl raised his ski pole from the drift and yelled out: 'Thanks, Hiro.'

On Wednesday, 10th May, we camped at 89 degrees 21 minutes North but were losing ground all the time as the pack continued to drift strongly south. To try to bring some order to my blurred existence I began sorting my sledge. My special things were ready for the Pole – Teddy; my Polar Medal and that of Edgar Evans of Scott's expedition; a tiny piece of rock from Antarctica; my piece of the *Discovery*, and gifts and mementos from those I loved.

As I slept that day I dreamt of Bleathgill, my cottage atop the moors in Cumbria. I could feel the golden light which poured across the grasses, could hear the wind bending the trees. In the valley I could see the ruins of Castle Brough rising from its hillock, above me I heard the call of ravens. The vision blurred into another and then another; I had disjointed images of Japan, Australia, the United States, Misha's home. I dreamt of all the homes I missed and I knew this was what I most looked forward to, returning home – wherever that was.

I awoke – I could not remember on which day – to a tremendous commotion coming from the tent. Darryl had refused to get out of his sleeping bag. He had climbed into it only minutes earlier after sitting about for several hours fiddling with his boots and pack. He had just managed to wrap the thing about his head when Gus woke up and roused the team. It was time to set out again. Darryl had hardly closed his eyes.

We marched for some hours and he turned to me and said: 'I think I feel sick.'

'Darryl, you're not sick', I said, 'you're exhausted. Now march.'

I continued to ski with Darryl, who sent a shock up my spine when suddenly he screamed, 'I can't go on!' But he did and I said nothing.

Graeme and Gus helped Misha through the leads; he was very proud of both and knew either could lead the group now if need be. In our exhaustion the team pulled together as never before and all the differences or problems we had had in the past seemed to melt away. Everyone pitched in to help Darryl and Hiro. When Darryl was struggling to cross an open lead, the ice moving all about him, Graeme dropped his pack and rushed back to pull him to safety. We worked

117 *Over page*: Rupert surveys the dark pools of water ahead

together to build bridges with our skis, following Misha's quiet instructions. He rarely put a foot wrong. We step-stoned across a wide lead, clambering on to a small floating piece of ice at its centre. The ice rocked and swayed as I, the last man, scrambled for safety. I would have gone in if Arved hadn't hauled me on to the floe.

On Thursday, 11th May, we managed fifteen miles and camped at 89 degrees 35 minutes. We slept hardly at all, and on Friday evening pushed ourselves out to twelve one-hour marches. Nineteen miles later we pitched camp six miles from the Pole. It was Saturday 13th May.

The journey was almost done, yet the thought of climbing into my sleeping bag was more delicious to me than laying siege to the Pole. We grinned through our exhaustion. Nothing could stop us now, except perhaps the Soviet stoves. They made one last effort to incinerate us after we had pitched camp.

We sat quietly in a huddle and dwelt on home. I thought of everyone who had made it possible for us to come this far. The list was long and I knew there were only two ways of saying thank you. One was to achieve the Pole, the other was not to waste that opportunity to draw attention to everything the expedition stood for – the need for international co-operation, whatever the difficulties, to protect the fragile Arctic and world environments.

118 A floating bridge

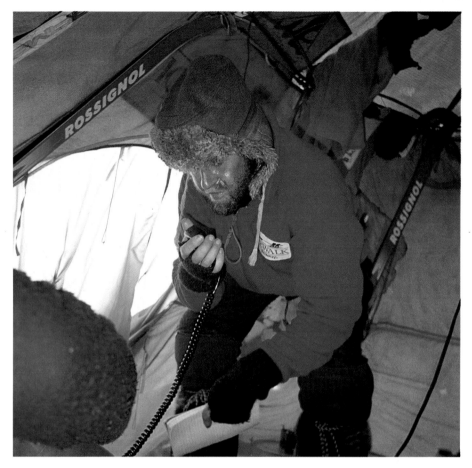

119 Rupert checks the satellite reading of the team's position

The further we travelled the more I nagged. 'For God's sake, don't go and get injured now.' In the back of my mind, the nearer we got to the Pole, there loomed the memory of the *Southern Quest*, sinking in minutes while Roger, Gareth and I were hauling our sledges that last mile in sight of the South Pole station. I knew we could not afford to count our chickens, and seemed powerless to stop the voice in my head repeating again and again those words I had scrawled in my diary three years ago: '. . . all hell has broken loose . . . the Pole experts will be rubbing their hands with glee to see our dreams strangled in newspaper headlines.' It was sapping my energy just when I most needed to be alert to our real situation here and now.

Foreboding of doom reached maniacal proportions as we prepared to set out again on Saturday evening for the last leg of our voyage. As I came to the end of an edgy kitchen duty with Rupert I found people outside the tent fumbling clumsily with gear and heard myself shouting hysterically: 'Look for crying out loud, we're six miles from the Pole; whatever you do, we don't want a lame duck at this stage!'

Everybody stared at me vacantly, as if I had finally gone mad. The spell was broken only when Rupert emerged to see what all the noise was about and uttered a sharp cry. Tripping on a fold in the tent, he had hopped to stay a fall and landed awkwardly with his boot in an unseen crack in the ice.

None of us could believe it. Six miles from the Pole and Rupert had twisted his ankle.

14

THE POLE

My heart pounded as I watched Misha carefully break open the packaging of a roller bandage.

'Rupert, Rupert – did ankle twist left or right?' he asked.

'Right,' Rupert winced.

The doctor nodded knowingly to himself, the statement apparently confirming a diagnosis already made. He set to work. The bandage seemed to flip from hand to hand as if the Russian were performing a conjuring trick instead of fashioning a support to control the swelling.

'Now, can you walk?' he said as Rupert eased the damaged joint into his boot.

I could only guess what was going through Rupert's mind. Anger at himself for getting injured this late in the journey? Concern, perhaps, that the Pole had been snatched from his grasp, or worse – that the entire team might have been hamstrung by one moment of bad luck? Or, I wondered, putting myself in his place, was he simply making a judgment on whether the last few miles would be worth the effort? As navigator, Rupert knew better than any of us that the North Pole exists only as a mathematical concept, the point at which lines of longitude converge. It was not the summit of a mountain on which he could fix his sights as we battled upwards, and when we got there he would not be able to plant a flag on the tangible apex of his achievement. But for all that, I knew what a profound landmark it was in Rupert's life. It was a prize that I myself would not have surrendered without a violent struggle.

Nor, apparently, would Rupert. After a few exploratory hobbles up and down the ice he swung his pack up on to his shoulders and adjusted the heavy weight on his back.

'I wouldn't make a habit of this,' he said through clenched teeth, but I don't think a few miles will hurt.'

He limped towards his sledge, strapped himself slowly into the harness, and gave Misha a determined nod of readiness. We were off.

We notched up what felt to me like four or five miles under a damp, grey curtain of cloud. I marched like a man possessed, driven now by panic. I began looking over my shoulder, for what I was not sure – a bear, a huge break in the ice threatening to engulf us. To be eaten by a polar bear in the last mile was surely no different from losing the *Southern Quest*? Maybe we were drastically off course. Why did everyone ahead keep stopping and fiddling with the radio? Why had Arved and Rupert yet again to consult their charts and take a fresh compass bearing?

Then I remembered. The Argos fix confirmed that we had drifted a full geographical mile during the hours of sleep, and were still moving to the south-east at a speed of 230 metres an hour. To compensate, Rupert's decision had been to make straight for the Pole, allowing for the drift, and to aim to go on a straight line for a short distance beyond it and thus to walk 'through' the Pole.

Ahead of me they stopped once more. As I drew up Rupert said quietly that he was sure we had arrived, but still he was receiving satellite positions short of the Pole. Compasses were checked, and we moved off again. In the blur that was my experience, I hardly took in at the next stop the ribald remarks that hung in the air as the last fix was corrected over the radio. We looked from one to the other – Arved, Misha, Graeme, Gus, Hiro. At first I did not register the expressions on their faces, though Darryl looked drunk with fatigue and pain. Then I realised, these were grins. This was not just another brief halt soon to end in more slog. We had passed through the place which was the North Pole and stood just on the Soviet side. Fifty-six days after setting foot on the ocean's surface, we were at the top of the world. It looked exactly like many other places we had seen along the way, and I didn't feel very much.

'Gentlemen,' Misha intoned, 'it seems to me that we should congratulate each other.'

I gazed at the heavy clouds looming on a bleak horizon and shivered involuntarily in the fresh breeze, despite the mild temperature of minus 11. If only the sun were there to greet us as it circled the sky without perceptibly rising or falling behind this blanket of mist.

'Oh, come on, let's get the bloody tent up,' someone muttered.

'But first we must do correct thing for each other,' Misha persisted, extending a shapeless gloved hand stiffly towards me. I clasped it with mine and put my other arm round his shoulder. Then came the tears as we all shook hands and embraced. Lightheadedness swept in. Eight rounds of ammunition were produced and eight volleys senselessly fired into the air by each of us in turn, in complete disregard of our ecological zeal. Flares were lit for no one to see but us. It was the closest we could come to a fireworks celebration. It was a release rather than any mark of exuberant achievement. Arved smoked a cigar, and before long almost everyone had collapsed into deep sleep in the tent.

I noted in my journal that the Pole was ours at 3.38 a.m. (local time) on Sunday, 14th May 1989. Then I went walking. It seemed I couldn't stop. My back hurt, and the pain that I had tried so hard to ignore these last few weeks suddenly rushed in as if a floodgate had been lifted. I limped across the snow, back to the point that was the Pole, and found a small slab of ice. I climbed on to it and spun around with my arms in the air, pointing – there's Britain, there's the United States, there's the Soviet Union. I spun around the world again and again.

I was at the North Pole. I could barely remember how I had got there, the journey was so blurred in my mind.

I felt very vulnerable, small and insignificant, imagining the world from space with me standing at its top on a lump of ice. Out there somewhere, someone could see a star which was our sun, and there I was standing at the top of a tiny little planet, 93 million miles away from that star. How pathetically small I was compared to the vastness above me. How alone was our planet, and how petty and stupid we all were.

For a brief moment I did catch a glimpse of our real situation – not a vision or a revelation, just an understanding.

Arved, too, felt something of what I saw, but everyone had his own experiences. For Rupert, it was a navigation triumph after all the years of planning and organisation. He had brought us, as he later wrote (see Appendix 1), to within 438 metres of the Pole, an even closer call than Roger's miraculous achievement in the South three years earlier. Darryl was relieved that the suffering, if for him not yet over, would not be increased any closer to breaking point. Hiro was almost in a coma, looking totally incapable of ever setting foot on Everest, let alone reaching its summit, as he was to do within a year. Graeme was proud, and deservedly so. Misha was pleased, and 'comfortable with our achievement.' Angus could only be thinking of home.

While we awaited evacuation, the weather worsened – cloud came down below 300 metres, with very poor contrast. I knew that any delay would throw the press conference into disarray. A Boeing 737, crammed with press reporters, was due to depart Ottawa for Resolute at any moment, and there is only so long you can keep eighty journalists waiting in a town without a pub.

121 Teddy – the first bear to have walked both Poles

Later that evening the weather began to clear. In the distance we could see a small aircraft approaching, but it wasn't ours. It was my dear old mates, Giles Kershaw and Dick Smith, on their way to the Soviet Union. They flew low over camp, waved and hurled a small survival package, including the latest Canadian newspapers, on to the ice.

Later a jet circled the Pole. It was the Amway team, and somewhere on board was my brother Charles.

In the early hours of Monday morning we had news from Eureka that the evacuation fleet was already on its way. We dismantled the tent and began to prepare our packs and the sledges for one final journey.

120 *Previous page*: The Pole at last!

Towards midday we heard a flotilla of aircraft advancing from the South. Three Twin Otters bounced to earth, disgorging journalists, and photographers, as well as Amway's Bill Nicholson with a jeroboam of vintage champagne.

'The Pole at last!!!' Admiral Robert Peary had written in his diary on 6th April, 1909. 'The prize of three centuries, my dream and ambition for twenty-three years.' He had built a snow cairn, left an account of his expedition in a glass bottle, written a postcard to his wife, raised the American flag, and turned for home.

Now this was our moment for sinking flags – the United Nations flag, flags from each of our home countries, flags from friends and supporters. We were photographed, filmed and interviewed. We drank champagne and saki and felt ill. Laughing and relaxed we loaded our equipment into the aircraft.

It was over.

When we were airborne I continued to glance over my shoulder – ever watchful for a last minute mishap. I could not breathe easily until we passed over land. I peered through the smudged aircraft window at the vast sea of ice below and could not believe we had crossed that endless maze of pressure ridges and open leads laid out so starkly and with such sinister intent.

122 Photographed waving the flags of all nations

124 Misha and Robert unwind on the flight back to Resolute Bay

Five hours later we landed in Eureka and transferred from the Twin Otters to a battered old DC3 that was to wing us south to Resolute. We touched down just before midnight and taxied towards the tiny terminal, the grand old aircraft bouncing gently.

Almost a hundred journalists and cameramen stood huddled in the cold. The door slid open and the press surged forward. Rupert disembarked first, looking tiny and puffy-faced; the team followed one by one. I climbed out last, holding my back straight as I tried to negotiate the aircraft steps. We were swarmed by a barrage of cameras and microphones. Family and friends hung to one side.

Ushered into the crowded airport terminal we took our places at a long press table beneath the blinding glare of television lights. After the white empty sameness of the Arctic, the light, movement, noise and smell of this room were almost overwhelming.

We leaned on the table towards the microphones, answering question after question. Misha and Graeme chatted animatedly. Gus looked pleased to be home. Arved and Hiro stared into space. Rupert smiled and Darryl grinned as he propped his hideously deformed foot on the table for the press to photograph. One of the journalists threw up.

Then followed twelve hours of live satellite television and radio interviews. As I stood in the snow and the howling wind, speaking to

123 *Previous page*: A bird's eye view of the hazards caused by the spring melt

125 A jubilant team faces the world's media

morning television hosts on the other side of the world, I thought I had never felt so cold or tired.

At midday on Tuesday we climbed into another aircraft and headed south to civilization proper. In Ottawa we were greeted by more journalists and temperatures in the high twenties. The shock of the heat was killing. We could walk only 300 metres before having to sit down and catch our breath. At the Pole I had felt pretty bad, but now my back was dreadful. I could barely walk.

I checked into a hotel, sat in a chair, took off my boots and had a bath. I ordered room service, toyed with my knife and fork and stared at the green of the trees outside the window. I glanced at my schedule. It appeared I was to visit Japan, the Soviet Union, the United States and Australia within ten days of arriving at the Pole. I slowly packed my bags and prepared to fly to London with my team to meet Margaret Thatcher. But first, there were just a few telephone calls to be made . . .

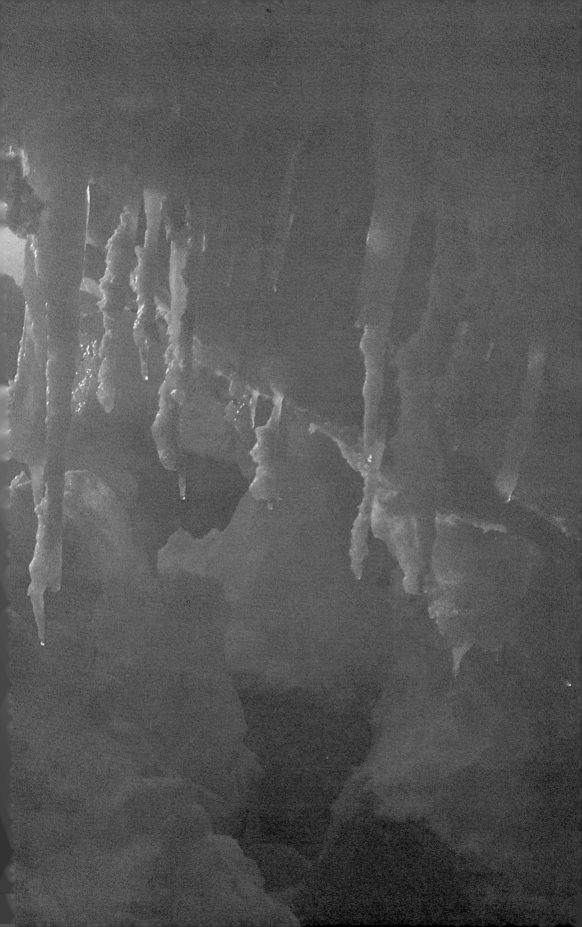

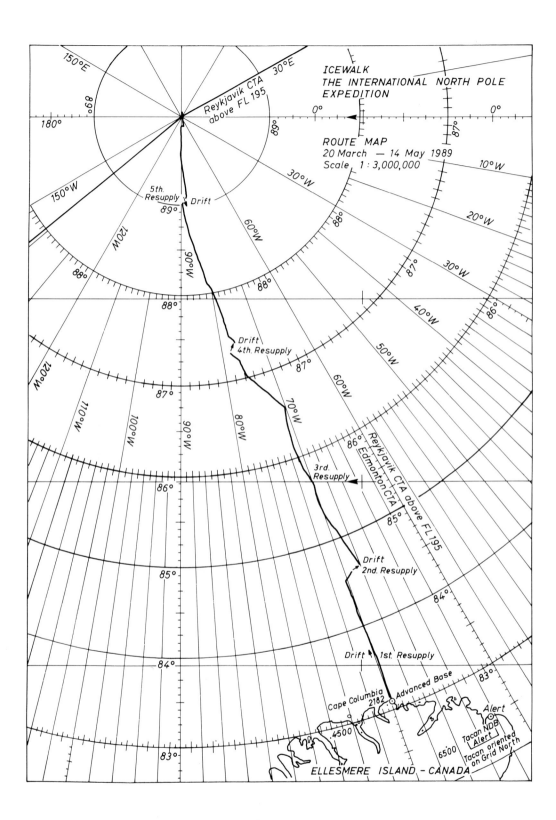

Appendix 1
ICEWALK NAVIGATION
by Rupert Summerson

First among a number of problems in Polar navigation is the position of the magnetic Poles, and their effect on the compass. The North Magnetic Pole is currently in the vicinity of Lougheed Island (77° 30′N 105° 00′W) in the Elizabeth Islands of Canada's high Arctic. At Cape Columbia (83° 06′N 70° 00′W) the magnetic declination (the angle between true north and magnetic north) is 83°W. For us this meant that at the start of our walk the compass needle pointed almost due west, and if you think of that as magnetic due north (or nearly) we were travelling – according to the compass – due east!

The horizontal field is very weak so close to the magnetic pole (only 600 miles to the south-west of our starting point) so the compass needles were very unsteady and took a long time to settle. As we moved north and further away from the magnetic Pole, the field became stronger and the compass steadier.

At the same time, the lines of longitude converge towards the Pole, as do the lines of magnetic declination. With the latter changing rapidly, it was crucial to know our longitude to find the correct declination. The traditional way to do this is to take a bearing on the sun at the same time as a sun sight and work out the magnetic declination from a calculated bearing of the sun at the time of the sight from your known position. To avoid wasting time on such a long procedure, I obtained from the Geophysics Division of the Geological Survey of Canada a map of magnetic declination and a computer-produced table of declination for each degree of latitude and longitude.

When I started to plan Icewalk I wanted to use only the traditional forms of navigation – sextant (or theodolite), tables, charts and compass. But in the end I recognised the over-riding need for a system that was lightweight, accurate and reliable, with back-up that would function whatever happened. If we were to succeed, in other words, we needed the best that was available today.

I chose Argos for our primary system. It had been recommended to me by Dr Jean-Louis Etienne who used it on his solo expedition to the North Pole in 1986. I myself had tried it on our reconnaissance expedition in 1987 and was impressed by its flexibility. The CAP-1 'Adventure' PTT (Platform Transmitting Terminal), made by Telonics Inc. in the United States, weighs 1.4 kg, measures 7 × 6 × 16 cm with a short whip antenna, and runs on sealed batteries that last for 60 days, 24 hours a day, at temperatures below minus 40 degrees celsius. We carried two of these platforms, in case one broke down, was lost or damaged, or the batteries ran out.

The Argos system works through 'Transit' satellites such as NOAA 7. As a satellite passes overhead, it interrogates the PTT, determines its position (from +/−1 km to +/−150 m) and collects any environmental data the PTT has to pass. The satellite then downloads the data on its next pass over its nearest ground station which is accessed into the Argos computer. The user can then access the Argos computer through an ordinary data link.

The CAP-1 has two important features in addition to its position-locating function. It has six switches: on/off, normal/emergency, and four code switches. The emergency switch, when thrown, will alert staff at the Argos centre, who in turn would alert someone nominated by the user and the Search and Rescue authority for the region where it is being used. In our case, that meant the Mounties.

The four code switches each have two positions so that it becomes possible to send a total of sixteen messages which are agreed in advance with headquarters. This feature was of particular importance to us. I knew that High Frequency radio communications were likely to be bad; in fact, they were the worst experienced in the Arctic for twenty years. Using the Argos, we could keep our headquarters informed, in general terms of how we were getting on. I could foresee that we might need a resupply when we were without radio communications. Radio blackouts can last for a week, by which time we could have starved. With Argos we could send a message about our local weather conditions. Here is the complete list of our codes.

Argos codes used by Icewalk

	S_1	S_2	S_3	S_4	Value appearing in Argos message	Meaning
	o	o	o	o	000	Conditions OK. Going well
1)	I	o	o	o	017	Conditions poor. Slow going
2)	o	I	o	o	034	Bad weather. Stationary
3)	I	I	o	o	051	Halted by open water/very thin ice
4)	o	o	I	o	068	Weather stable. Good for resupply
5)	I	o	I	o	085	Weather changeable. Resupply possible
6)	o	I	I	o	102	Weather poor. Resupply not possible
7)	I	I	I	o	119	* Turn on radio ● Radio broken
8)	o	o	o	I	136	* Require fuel & food ● Require tent/s
	I	o	o	I	153	* Require resupply on time ● Require sleeping bags
	o	I	o	I	170	* Require resupply x days early ● Require skis/bindings
	I	I	o	I	187	Switch to number
	o	o	I	I	204	Minor injury or fatigue but moving on
	I	o	I	I	221	Injury requiring evacuation but can wait until resupply
	o	I	I	I	238	One or more injured require plane as soon as possible
	I	I	I	I	255	Require immediate assistance

Notes: 1) etc. in left hand column is the number of days, items, etc.
        * PTT number 163   ● PTT number 162

The Argos computer was accessed by Jeremy Morris, our Liaison Officer at Resolute Bay – the end of the telephone line. Using an Apple computer and Modem, he would access the Argos computer in Toulouse just before the time set for the next radio schedule with the Polar team. When he established communications with the Polar team, either direct or most commonly through our Advanced Base at Cape Columbia, he would pass on our position.

Our positions were thus always known to our support staff, so that if we had an accident, rescue aircraft would know where to locate us. The code system was extremely valuable when communications were poor, and meant that despite non-existent radio communications, we could always let our support staff know we were all right. The system is also very accurate: a grade 3 position gives an accuracy of $+/-$ 150 m. I found this to be very helpful in tracking the speed and direction of the drift of the ice, particularly at the North Pole.

The great disadvantage of the system is that we had to rely on external help to obtain our position. Although the system helped us to keep in touch when radio communications were poor, conversely we were unable to receive our position when the radio link failed. For this reason, I selected celestial navigation as our back-up method – sextant with an artificial horizon, calculator and sight-reduction tables. I measured distance in nautical miles – which is, after all, what you would expect for navigation across an ocean! Without being too pedantic, a nautical mile is near enough to a minute of latitude, and there are sixty in one degree. Other team members were less familiar with nautical miles and so at the beginning I converted them into statute miles for some (1 nautical mile = 1.152 statute miles) and into kilometres for others (1 nautical mile = 1.8532 kilometres). By the end of the journey everyone knew what a nautical mile was, and if conditions were good you could travel two of them in an hour.

The sextant I used was an Ebbco Standard, which is cheap and made of plastic. This was not my first choice but came about by chance. Arved Fuchs, an experienced navigator, had recently bought a C. Plath sextant with a bubble attachment. He had paid 5,000 DM for it, and it came in a beautiful wooden case weighing about 5 kg, and so Arved bought an aluminium camera case to put it in. Unfortunately, when the time came to pack his sledge he could not fit the camera case in, and since he did not want to carry 5 kg of wood to the Pole, we had to leave his sextant behind. In contrast, the Ebbco is very light, but it did not like the extreme cold, and as it shrank it became very loose and developed an index error of 17'. I tried to correct it, but found that it was just too difficult using the tiny Allen key with gloves.

The artificial horizon was made by Zeiss-Freiberger in East Germany. It comprised a circular piece of smoked glass set in a circular frame with three levelling screws at 120° to each other. To level it, you used two spirit levels set at right angles to each other laid on the glass. These were removed when levelling was complete. I made the mistake of taking them out of their box to save weight, wrapping them in pieces of closed cell foam instead. When I had a very heavy fall skiing off a pressure ridge I broke one of the spirit levels. It was still possible to level with one, but it took twice as long. The artificial horizon worked very well, designed as it is for use in the cold with large levelling screws and the stalks on the spirit levels show. It is important to have a good solid surface on which to set it. I had hoped to use just a flat piece of wood laid on the snow but it tended to skid about, so I resorted to an aluminium case with feet.

The calculator was a Hewlett-Packard HP-41 CV with a Hewlett-Packard Navigation programme or pac. I found it very useful not only for sight reduction, but also for aligning the radio antenna using the great-circle function, and for general calculations, such as adding up weights for aircraft loading. There is another programme called the Bobby Schenk Navigation pac which Arved had in his calculator (also a Hewlett-Packard). This enabled two or more sights to be combined and an observed position determined without having to plot them. Despite temperatures of well below minus 40°C, with a bit of warming the calculator worked well.

Our compasses were Silva Model 15TD. This model has a declination ring to which you set the compass needle. This was useful when the declination ranged from 90° to 130° West.

Most of the route-finding was done by Misha Malakhov, the Soviet doctor. It was not possible to move on a given bearing because the magnetic field is very weak in high latitudes, so he, Graeme Joy and Angus Cockney would simultaneously take a bearing on a prominent lump of ice in the distance and then we would make our way to it. Because the ice was rough and we were constantly having to make detours, and also because the ice was drifting, it was not worth having any form of distance measuring device like Robert Swan had on his expedition to the South Pole. There they used a wheel attached to the sledge which clicked up the kilometres like a bicycle mileometer.

Other navigational equipment I carried were a fabulously accurate watch – the Yema Spationaute III, which did not lose or gain a second during the whole journey; the Nautical Almanac with all but the most relevant pages cut out (I kept the sight reduction tables in the back in case the calculator broke); a Douglas protractor; a twelve inch ruler; a propelling pencil; and a pair of dividers. Although the dividers were quite heavy, and I could have used the ruler, they were well worth their weight in time saved on the journey.

The map I used was specially drawn up by Arved Fuchs' girlfriend. It covered the whole of the journey from Cape Columbia to the North Pole, and a bit beyond, at 1:500,000 scale. It was drawn on Polar Stereographic projection, and it proved very useful to have just one map.

When we arrived at the North Pole, we were sent a GPS satellite navigator. This uses the new generation of geostationary satellites, as opposed to the orbiting transit satellites. It measured about 30×20×10 cm and weighed about 1 kg, with the antenna built into its box. Earlier models I had seen were four times the size and weighed five times as much.

This device was truly incredible. I am still debating with myself whether we should have taken a GPS instead of the second Argos, but what then would have happened if the first Argos had failed? Should we have taken it instead of the sextant? But what would have happened if the GPS had failed? I maintain that one should always have a failsafe back-up that will always work.

Our main problem was quite obvious when you look at the map of our journey and the big deviation west. As I mentioned, 1989 was the worst year for sunspot activity and magnetic storms in twenty years. The Arctic coast of northern Canada is close to the North Magnetic Pole; there the lines of magnetic variation are nearly parallel to the lines of longitude, and are as closely spaced. The lines of magnetic variation change as rapidly as one degree for every degree of longitude. It is therefore crucial to know your longitude, for during severe magnetic storms fluctuations may exceed six degrees. Thus, even when you know your longitude, your compass setting may be up to six degrees out. We found ourselves deviating west, and, however much we tried to compensate, for days we still headed north-west instead of north. How much was due to drifting ice, and how much to magnetic storms I do not know.

A further problem arose when we lost radio communications in these magnetic storms and I had to obtain our position by celestial navigation. I was mistaken in thinking, as I did at first, that only latitude was important. If one kept heading north eventually you would reach the Pole, I reasoned – but north is only where you calculate it. I soon discovered that longitude was more important, and longitude, as all navigators know, is far more difficult to obtain. In tropical regions one can estimate the longitude by timing the sun's meridian passage. In the Polar regions this will not work – the higher the latitude the flatter the sun's trajectory. At one time I was lucky in that both the sun and the moon were visible at the same time and high enough to use the artificial horizon. I was thus able to get an observed position from intersecting position lines. At other times only the sun was visible.

I felt it was a waste of time taking a sight for latitude at midday and then running on the position line to a sight taken in the evening at camp. The distance to be run on would only be an educated guess, and so would the course. What do you get when you use two guesses? What I really needed was a sight for longitude only. Taking a sight when the sun is on the prime vertical is not usually satisfactory because it is often too low to enable one to use an artificial horizon.

How, too, do you know it is on the prime vertical when you need to take a bearing and you are taking the sight to find your longitude so you know what the magnetic variation is to apply to the bearing so you will know what that bearing is? My solution was to stay in one place and take a number of well spaced sights of the sun, preferably two with a six-hour interval. If one of these could be a noon sight, so much the better. In that way one does not have to take a sight specifically for longitude. The problem with this method is that as the season progresses and the pack-ice breaks up, the increasing amount of low cloud makes sun shots increasingly difficult, and one has to be ready to drop everything to snatch a shot.

The problem of defining what exactly our North Pole would be was the subject of much discussion, and the prevailing opinion was that we should get 'as close as possible'. It seemed that 89° 59′N would be easily possible but as we approached the Pole I wondered if we should go for 89° 59.9999′.

Two other factors came into force: time, and the need to find an ice-floe suitable as an airstrip. Given a week, we might even have got 90° 00′. With a press conference arranged for us in Resolute on 14th May, we had to compromise between an indisputable North Pole and the amount of time left. A further factor made itself known during the 'night' of 12/13th May, after which we received five positions showing a very strong current parallel to the 20°W meridian at 0.125 nautical miles per hour (230 metres per hour).

A number of solutions seemed possible; we could make for a point beyond the Pole on 160°E meridian and drift back across it, then box it, or make straight for the Pole allowing for the drift and aim to go on a straight line a short distance beyond it, and thus we could be said to have walked 'through' the Pole. We chose the latter.

We set off from 89° 53′N 69° 11′W at 3.30 a.m. UT on 14th May.

At each hourly rest stop, we received our latest satellite position which by then was about 110 minutes old. We kept the Argos switched on all the time, so that the only delay would be in the satellite and processing at Argos.

At 8.22 a.m. UT on 14th May we were at 89° 59.28′N 69° 33.72′W, and at 10.04 a.m. UT we were at 89° 59.22′N 69° 09.84′E. We had passed by the Pole by 438 metres. Good enough!

Adapted from Rupert Summerson's article
in *Navigation News* (Vol. 1, Issue 6),
published by the Royal Institute of Navigation, Dec. 1989.

Appendix 2
DAILY LOG OF THE ICEWALK EXPEDITION
1989

The log is arranged as follows: the day number refers to the period actually spent travelling or to a period of rest. Therefore, on travelling days, the day number is next to the start time, which is the upper of a pair of numbers. The lower time is the finish time. Interspersed between the 'days' are the numbers of campsites. The resupply periods invariably took up extra days, waiting for aircraft, carrying medical research and resting. Although the journey took 56 calendar days, because we finished the journey during the night of the last day and because of our peculiar sleep and travel patterns we appear to have lost a day.

Latitudes and longitudes are given in degrees, minutes and decimals of a minute, and are respectively north and west unless otherwise specified.

The temperatures are given in pairs, the highest (first) and lowest some time during a period, normally while camping.

The surface of the Arctic Ocean, while frozen, is not frozen into one solid mass. Instead, it is formed by an infinite number of bits, called floes. These move around under the influence of winds and currents. If the drift is in a northerly direction, obviously it is helpful, and if it is moving southwards, it is carrying us away from our goal. The drift is only plottable while we are stationary, but it is also moving while we are.

Miles given are nautical miles, or minutes of latitude or equivalent. One nautical mile equals 1.8532 kilometres or 1.152 statute miles. The bearing given is the course achieved between the two campsites. The closer to 360° the better, but deflection either side of that figure could be due to such diverse factors as drifting ice, difficult going and diversions round leads of open water. Severe magnetic storms would have affected our compasses, also causing deflection.

Argos system accuracy. Positions given by Argos are graded 1, 2 or 3. A Grade 1 position is accurate to $+/-1$ kilometre, Grade 2 $+/-250$ metres and Grade 3 $+/-150$ metres. Where possible Grade 2 or 3 positions have been selected in the chart if they are at more or less the times given, otherwise Grade 1 positions are given.

Total distance travelled 433.0 nautical miles = 498.8 statute miles. The distance by ruler from Cape Columbia to the North Pole is 414 nautical or 477 statute miles. The expedition therefore travelled a distance 4.6% more than was necessary. The average daily mileage was 7.73 nautical miles if the distance is divided among 56 days or, if it is divided by the 44 days actually travelled, the average is 9.84 nautical or 11.34 statute miles.

The distances given are measured in a straight line from the position given and the time of starting the day's travel to the position of the following evening's campsite and do not take into account the turns left and right to avoid this lead of open water and to find an easier crossing point over that pressure ridge. Wally Herbert, Britain's most experienced Arctic traveller, in his excellent analysis of Peary, *The Noose of Laurels*, estimates that one makes detours adding up to increased mileage of an extra 25%. In the light of our experience that would seem to be reasonable and would make our total distance 541.25 nautical or 623.52 statute miles (998 kilometres). If you add to this an estimated 2,000 pressure ridges at an average height of 5 metres, which gives a combined height of 10,000 metres I think that the journey now starts to assume its correct perspective.

Icewalk
Travel log

Day	Date	Time	Lat. (N)	Long. (W)	Temp.	Drift/miles	Miles travelled	Magnetic variation
1	20/3	1430	83°06.5′	69°40.6′	(Start)			
	20/3	1905	83°11.8	69°46.3			5.3 @ 353°	83°W
	Camp 1							
2	20/3	2230	83°09.5	69°37.4	−37h/−42l	2.5 @ 155°		
	21/3	1714	83°19.0	69°50.6			9.6 @ 351°	83°
	Camp 2							
3	22/3	0658	83°15.8	69°36.0	−36h/−44l	3.6 @ 152°		
	22/3	1844	83°20.0	69°51.8			4.6 @ 336°	83°
	Camp 3							
4	23/3	0505	83°21.7	69°45.0	−40h/−42l	1.9 @ 025°		
	23/3	1834	83°25.8	70°00.8			4.5 @ 336°	83°
	Camp 4							
5	24/3	0957	83°26.9	69°49.4	−36h/−42l	1.7 @ 050°		
	24/3	1903	83°33.1	70°00.4			6.3 @ 349°	84°
	Camp 5							
6	25/3	0834	83°35.9	69°44.8	−41h/−52l	3.3 @ 032°		
	25/3	1957	83°41.2	69°53.8			5.4 @ 349°	84°
	Camp 6							
7	26/3	1003	83°41.5	70°01.0	−38h/−42l	0.8 @ 291°		
	26/3	2129	83°40.8	69°55.1			No travelling	
	Camp 6							
8	27/3	1254	83°41.1	69°55.2	−41h/−44l	Position update No travelling		
	Camp 6					Resupply 1		
9	28/3					No position update No travelling		
	Camp 6							
10	29/3	2057	83°41.2	69°56.8	−40h/−41l	Position update no travelling		
	Camp 6					0.3 @ 270°(Total drift)		
11	30/3					No position for start of travel		
	30/3	2051	83°46.8	69°48.6			5.7 @ 009°	84°
	Camp 7							
12	31/3	0629	83°46.4	70°03.7	−37h/−42l	1.7 @ 256°		
	31/3	1854	83°54.0	69°52.4			7.7 @ 009°	84°
	Camp 8							
13	1/4	0922	83°54.2	69°55.6	−36h/−39l	0.4 @ 300°		
	1/4	1844	84°01.3	70°06.4			7.2 @ 351°	84°
	Camp 9							

14	2/4	0908	84°02.2	70°09.6	−34h/−38l	1.0 @ 340°		
	2/4	1832	84°04.7	70°12.7			2.5 @ 353°	85°
	Camp 10							
15	3/4	0704	84°04.9	70°11.6	−36h/−43l	0.2 @ 030°		
	3/4	2024	84°13.4	70°25.7			8.6 @ 350°	85°
	Camp 11							
16	4/4	0641	84°13.1	70°26.6	−38h/−41l	0.3 @ 197°		
	4/4	2143	84°23.8	70°39.3			10.8 @ 353°	85°
	Camp 12							
17	5/4	0618	84°23.2	70°27.8	−37h/−39l	1.3 @ 118°		
	5/4	2119	84°33.1	70°36.7			9.9 @ 355°	86°
	Camp 13							
18	6/4	0921	84°33.5	70°12.7	−37h/−39l	2.3 @ 080°		
	6/4	1935	84°37.6	69°39.7			5.1 @ 037°	86°
	Camp 14							
19	7/4	1925	84°40.0	68°37.4	−21h/−29l	Representative position after 24 hours No travelling bad weather		
	Camp 14							
20	8/4	1914	84°40.6	68°12.7	−27h/−33l	No travelling Resupply 2		
	Camp 14							
21	9/4	1903	84°40.9	68°13.0	−33h/−39l	No travelling		
	Camp 14							
22	10/4	1421	84°40.0	68°13.4	−37h/−41l	8.4 @ 073°(Total drift)		
	10/4	2109	84°45.3	68°33.5			6.5 @ 341°	86°
	Camp 15							
23	11/4	0726	84°44.6	68°15.7	−39h/−41l	1.8 @ 113°		
	11/4	2026	84°57.4	68°21.5			12.8 @ 358°	86°
	Camp 16							
24	12/4	0659	84°55.1	68°29.0	−38h/−44l	2.4 @ 196°		
	12/4	2157	85°05.5	68°52.6			10.6 @ 349°	86°
	Camp 17							
25	13/4	0957	85°03.8	69°06.7	−30h/−37l	2.1 @ 215°		
	13/4	2143	85°09.7	69°28.1			6.2 @ 343°	87°
	Camp 18							
26	14/4	0619	85°09.8	69°30.6	−30h/−32l	0.2 @ 295°		
	14/4	2122	85°15.5	69°25.1			5.7 @ 005°	87°
	Camp 19							
27	15/4	0756	85°16.9	69°51.1	−21h/−25l	2.6 @ 303°		
	15/4	2124	85°24.7	70°17.6			8.1 @ 345°	88°
	Camp 20							
28	16/4	0714	85°25.4	70°03.8	−22h/−25l	1.3 @ 058°		
	16/4	2030	85°34.4	70°08.4			9.0 @ 358°	88°
	Camp 21							
29	17/4	0735	85°34.0	70°06.7	−26h/−34l	0.4 @ 162°		
	17/4	1235	85°36.5	70°12.4		Resupply 3	2.5 @ 350°	89°
	Camp 22							
30	18/4	0953	85°41.0	70°19.4	−11h/−29l	4.5 @ 353°		
	18/4	2237	85°46.7	70°33.5			5.8 @ 350°	89°
	Camp 23							
31	19/4	0857	85°47.0	70°29.3	−25h/−27l	0.4 @ 046°		
	19/4	2110	85°54.0	70°59.6			7.3 @ 343°	90°
	Camp 24							
32	20/4	0900	85°54.3	70°54.4	−25h/−28l	0.5 @ 051°		
	20/4	2216	86°05.2	71°17.0			11.0 @ 352°	91°
	Camp 25							
33	21/4	0834	86°05.1	71°17.9	−25h/−26l	0.1 @ 212°		
	21/4	2003	86°20.2	71°42.8			15.2 @ 354°	91°
	Camp 26							
34	22/4	0644	86°20.0	71°40.6	−24h/−26l	0.2 @ 145°		
	22/4	2145	86°33.2	72°45.4			13.8 @ 343°	92°
	Camp 27							

35	23/4 0804	86°33.5	73°15.2	−18h/−26l	1.8 @ 280°		
	23/4 2122	86°47.2	74°47.6			14.7 @ 339°	93°
	Camp 28						
36	24/4 0804	86°47.2	75°10.7	−20h/−21l	1.3 @ 270°		
	24/4 2241	87°01.0	75°21.7			13.8 @ 358°	97°
	Camp 29						
37	25/4 0755	87°00.3	75°36.9	−15h/−18l	1.1 @ 229°		
	25/4 2213	87°11.2	76°21.4			11.1 @ 348°	100°
	Camp 30						
38	26/4 0919	87°11.6	76°19.7	−12h/−18l	0.4 @ 012°		
	26/4 2112	87°18.1	77°23.6			7.2 @ 335°	101°
	Camp 31				Resupply 4		
39	27/4 2101	87°18.2	77°7.7	−20h/−23l	Representative position		
	Camp 31				No travel		
40	28/4 2111	87°20.0	76°20.7	−15h/−24l	Representative position		
	Camp 31				No travel		
41	29/4 0221	87°20.6	76°27.1	−15h/−24l	3.6 @ 047°(Total drift)		
	29/4 1406	87°32.6	76°39.7			12.0 @ 357°	102°
	Camp 32						
42	30/4 0200	87°30.4	76°57.8	−21h/−29l	2.3 @ 200°		
	30/4 1705	87°45.8	77°41.0			15.5 @ 353°	103°
	Camp 33						
43	1/5 0146	87°45.7	77°50.8	−20h/−22l	0.4 @ 255°		
	1/5 1823	88°00.0	79°27.8			14.7 @ 346°	103°
	Camp 34						
44	2/5 0432	88°00.3	79°38.5	−21h/−22l	0.5 @ 309°		
	2/5 1942	88°12.2	81°58.6			12.8 @ 339°	108°
	Camp 35						
45	3/5 0632	88°12.4	83°06.9	−8h/−16l	2.1 @ 275°		
	3/5 2146	88°28.0	83°41.1			15.6 @ 356°	110°
	Camp 36						
46	4/5 1038	88°27.7	84°25.2	−5h/−13l	1.2 @ 256°		
	5/5 0058	88°39.0	85°58.1			11.5 @ 348°	113°
	Camp 37						
47	5/5 1157	88°39.1	86°37.7	−6h/−9l	0.9 @ 276°		
	6/5 0233	88°55.0	87°58.3			16.0 @ 354°	116°
	Camp 38						
48	6/5 1819	88°54.3	89°31.6	−8h/−14l	1.9 @ 248°		
	7/5 0725	89°05.6	89°13.1			11.3 @ 002°	119°
	Camp 39						
49	8/5 0720	89°03.6	90°02.3	−2h/−7l	Representative position		
	Camp 39				Resupply 5		
50	9/5 0023	89°01.4	90°53.0	−4h/−8l	4.5 @ 201°(Total drift)		
	9/5 1900	89°06.2	85°51.5			6.9 @ 046°	122°
	Camp 40						
51	10/5 0701	89°05.4	85°59.0	−1h/−5l	0.8 @ 188°		
	10/5 2329	89°19.2	86°44.3			13.8 @ 357°	120°
	Camp 41						
52	11/5 1155	89°17.6	86°54.4	−7h/−12l	1.6 @ 184°		
	12/5 0309	89°35.1	91°59.3			17.7 @ 351°	120°
	Camp 42						
53	12/5 1504	89°34.4	89°04.7	−12h/−16l	1.5 @ 117°		
	13/5 0623	89°54.1	81°18.8			19.8 @ 005°	122°
	Camp 43						
54	13/5 2225	89°53.1	69°11.2	−12h/−15l	1.7 @ 126°		
	14/5 0324	89°59.3	67°07.0W			(6.2 @ 001°)	
	14/5 0432	89°59.1	108°09.6E (End of travel)			10.9 @ 057°	120°
	Camp 43						
55	15/5 0812	89°57.8	29°57.1E		2.4 @ 237°	(Last position)	

Appendix 3
ICEWALK LOGISTICS
by Christine McCabe

'Few expeditions have imposed such intense pressures and demands over such a long period of time . . .'

Jim Hargreaves, Expedition and Logistics Manager

In late January 1989, Jim Hargreaves took possession of a basement office in a three-storied house in the suburbs of Ottawa – as unlikely an expedition headquarters as one could imagine. He was joined by Icewalk's support and base camp teams – an unusual assortment of people selected, almost haphazardly by the expedition's globe-trotting leader. They arrived in the midst of a bleak Canadian winter from all over the world – some seasoned Polar travellers, others getting their first taste of the cold. They had less than three weeks in which to convert their pleasant home into an efficient operational headquarters and prepare the eight-man Icewalk team for its final training session in Iqaluit and eventual manhaul to the North Pole.

Although the Icewalk North Pole expedition had been some three years in the planning the chaotic nature and rapidity of its growth, from a simple four-man assault on the Pole to an eight-man international endeavour and related student project, spelled one thing – a logistical nightmare.

It was not that Icewalk was ill-planned; in fact Rupert Summerson had worked steadily on the project's logistical requirements since the beginning. However the international diversity of the expedition and last minute growth into a mammoth media event, meant that only weeks before setting out, Icewalk was hard pressed to meet the deadline. For one thing the walkers were scattered across seven countries, precipitating a series of almost independent pre-expedition programmes.

The enormity of bringing together the logistical support requirements in Ottawa, accumulating equipment, sorting it, deciding what was suitable and what inadequate, and then making up the differences proved a herculean task. Food rations for 480 man-days had to be purchased, weighed, and packaged, in preparation for resupply or air drop, and assembled in Resolute Bay. Equipment had to be tested, clothing adjusted, and a comprehensive medical programme devised between the expedition's Soviet contingent and the Ottawa General Hospital.

Besides managing all these practicalities, Icewalk mounted a 24-hours per day media campaign: film crews were fitted out to withstand the rigours of the polar environment; cameras winterised and dozens of flights and charters co-ordinated to transport a large international press contingent back and forth across the Arctic. The difficulty of this complicated exercise was exacerbated by the fact that the expedition was running behind schedule – both men and equipment arrived in Canada far later than originally anticipated. The team's month-long February reconnoitre in Iqaluit became all the more essential to iron out the many logistical problems which emerged daily. There was all too little time for field training – their hours were consumed with the testing of polar equipment and the preparation of food and resupply packages.

Clothing arrived from Australia, Japan, Britain, the USA, the Soviet Union and elsewhere; tents from Moscow; sleeping bags from Queensland; skis from Vancouver; sledges from London. A circle of Inuit women on Broughton Island made sealskin Kamiks; local people adapted the team's Polar clothing along traditional Inuit lines. Sledge builders were flown from London to redesign amphibious prototypes as a precaution against the early break-up of the ice pack. Journalists and film crews came and went assembling documentary and publicity material.

In mid-March, as the media campaign built to a frantic pre-expedition crescendo and an exhausted logistics team drew breath after weeks of frenetic work, the Polar team set off from Iqaluit in their jammed Boeing 748 bound for Eureka on Baffin Island and the final leg of their journey. Five Twin otter flights were required to transfer all men, equipment and the film crew from Eureka to advance base at Cape Columbia, Canada's northernmost tip.

On 20th March, as the team took their first tentative steps towards the Pole, the 'fun' began for the support crews. The supply line, which extended beyond Ottawa to many points around the world needed 24-hour monitoring and had tremendous demands placed upon it. Appalling radio communications made the task of the support team even more difficult. On one occasion Jim Hargreaves was forced to telephone London from Ottawa, obtain a direct link to the Marine Communications System at Portishead and from there a link to Sir Ranulph Fiennes' base camp on Ward Hunt Island. Ward Hunt was able to effect a 'patch' to the polar team and Jim spoke to the Icewalk adventurers by telephone.

Such tales of ingenuity were not uncommon. The expedition was to require every ounce of resourcefulness and energy the base camp team could muster. As the polar walkers advanced north, so the supply line grew longer and more difficult to service. Every radio schedule included requests for some form of equipment or supply but no problem went unsolved.

Five separate resupply flights (excluding the North Pole evacuation) had to be timed to coincide with favourable weather. A fuel cache laid at 86 degrees 30 minutes north, suitable landing strips located and prepared by the polar team, and the pilots' flying hours had also to be taken into consideration. Given these variables it was almost impossible to fix a charter, and most resupply flights developed into nail-biting manoeuvres as pilots dodged and darted between breaks in the weather. With so many flights departing in such adverse conditions the risk factor was very high particularly during the final North Pole evacuation. The Arctic gives rise to some of the most unpredictable and dangerous flying conditions in the world. Fortunately it is also home to some of the world's best pilots. To a large degree the team's well being depended on their skill and experience.

The pressure to secure the team's safety as they battled north was immense, and no sooner had the Polar team set off than 22 students from 15 nations arrived, and together with a massive entourage were assembled, equipped and dispatched to 80 degrees north. At one point Ottawa HQ was co-ordinating the movement of more than seventy personnel at various points throughout the Arctic.

Every day brought new problems and new challenges, from locating special skis and inflatable rafts, to transporting eighty journalists from around the world to tiny Resolute Bay, from installing telephone lines in this remote settlement to transmitting satellite news broadcasts worldwide.

The expedition's final air movement scenario was Icewalk's most complicated manoeuvre. One 737, one DC3, three Twin Otters, eight men stranded by bad weather at the North Pole, eighty journalists stranded in Resolute Bay, three pilots poised for take-off in Eureka, and television stations all over the world awaiting pre-scheduled satellite feeds. The base camp team waited impatiently. Jim sat hunched in a small tent in Eureka speaking to the team on an hourly basis. Suddenly the cloud lifted, the Polar team gave the all clear, Jim said go, and the three Twin Otters scrambled swiftly for the Pole.

And so the expedition drew to a dramatic and very public close. For 56 long days the support team had battled through radio blackouts and appalling weather, chased lost cargo, and dealt with financial and media demands from the furthest corners of the earth. For the most part their dedication and resourcefulness went unsung. In many ways the Polar team was cocooned in a simple world – the hardships and suffering endured at base were every bit as consequential as those survived by the eight adventurers.

The Polar team's story is one of courage and determination, but their story would not have been possible without the dedication and support of an international back-up crew and hundreds of people around the world who hauled every step of the long journey with them.

Appendix 4
EQUIPMENT LIST FOR THE ICEWALKERS

The equipment taken varied considerably from person to person according to responsibilities, experience, needs and inclination. It also varied from time to time through the journey according to such factors as weather and temperature, the time of year and our development as a team.

Clothing

This was the most varied of all and reflected personal needs and inclinations most. What is included here is intended to be the most detailed list but it does not mean that everyone wore everything all the time.

Headwear

Fur hats (made from Arctic fox)	Made in the Soviet Union
Fleece hat	Trailhead
Fleece headband	Trailhead
Fibre-pile balaclava	Helly-Hansen
Ear-muffs	Swix
Neoprene face mask	
Headover	Norwegian Army type

Underwear

Personal or polypropylene underpants	
Thermal underwear, one or two piece, woollen or polypropylene	Dunlop, Helly-Hansen

Midwear

One-piece fibre-pile or fleece suit	Helly-Hansen or personal
Fleece salopettes	Karrimor
Fibre-pile or fleece jacket	Karrimor or Helly-Hansen

Outerwear

Windproof jackets ⎫	Made of Goretex by Mountain
Windproof salopettes ⎬	Designs
Duvet jackets	Mountain Designs

Gloves

Thin polypropylene gloves	All gloves were supplied by Paris Sport
Woollen gloves	
Fibre-pile mitts	

(Gloves continued)
Windproof mitts
Insulated gloves
Heavily insulated mitts
Wristlets

Footwear
Thin polypropylene socks   Fox River
Vapour barrier socks   Fairydown
Polarplus socks: All Polarplus socks made by High
   Short single   Tops Equipment
   Long single
   Long double with Thinsulate filling
Insoles   Surefoot Corporation
Kamiks (traditional Inuit sealskin boots) Made by the Minguk Sewing Circle
Camp boots   Broughton Is. NWT

Sunglasses and Goggles
Sunglasses (Spectra-Irex)   Bollé
Goggles (Irex 100)   Bollé

Sleeping Bags
Double bags, downfilled   Mountain Designs
Vapour barrier bags   Mountain Designs
Sleeping mats   Karrimat, Ajungilak, Cascade Designs

Skis
Ramer Grand Tour (4 pairs)   Alpine Research Inc.
Rossignol TMS (4 pairs)   Rossignol
Bindings   Berwin
Poles   Leki
Ski wax   Swix

Rucksacks and Sledges
Rucksacks   Karrimor Condor 60–80
Sledges   Norca toboggans
Sledges   Arved's design pulled by Arved & Robert
Sledge harnesses   Wilderness Equipment
Karabiners   Salewa

Camping Equipment
Soviet tent   Specially made in USSR
Australian tent   Half-sized copy made by Wilderness
                                        Equipment
Pyramid tent   Wilderness Equipment
Shovels (3)   Ramer
Snow saw   Camp
Stoves   MSR X-GK, Soviet 'Wasp', Coleman
                                        double burner
Candles   (At beginning)

(*Camping Equipment continued*)
Alcohol (Soviet stove primer)
Billies (2)   Trailhead
Wooden boards (to stand cookers on) (2)
Cigarette lighters
Matches
Spoon (1) each
Mug 750ml stainless steel   (Misha & Arved used a bowl as
Bowls   well as a mug)
Vacuum flask (1.5 litres) (2)   Aladdin
Ladles (2)
Lavatory paper
Toothpaste   Amway
Anti-perspirant stick   Amway

Fuel
Fuel cans 5 & 10 litre
Petrol   (For Soviet stoves)
White gas (Naphtha)   (For MSRs)

Fuel consumption was calculated at 1 litre per man per day for the start and then decreased

Communications
HF radios   Codan, Spilsbury
SARBE beacon (2)   FKI Instruments
Lithium batteries   Saft
Other batteries   various

Safety
Flares – Smoke & 2 Star
Heliograph
Rope (40m × 5mm)
Rifle (.270 calibre)
Ammunition (20 rounds)
Whistles

Navigation
Argos transmitter (2)   Telonics Inc.
Plastic sextant   Ebbco
Artificial horizon   Zeiss-Freiberger
Navigation calculator   Hewlett-Packard HP 41 CV
Map   1:500,000 specially made
Map and table of Magnetic Variation   Energy, Mines and Resources Canada
Compasses (8)   Silva Type 15T
Nautical Almanac, extracts
Ruler, pencil, dividers

Watches
North Pole, Spationaute III and II   CGH/Yema
Rallye II, Navygraf II

Tools and Spares

Knives	Victorinox (Swiss Army)
Ice axe	Choulnard
Hacksaw	Stanley minihack
Screwdrivers	
Jubilee clips (repairing broken ski poles)	
Adjustable wrench (for tightening fuel bottle lids)	
Spare pole baskets	
Spare baskets	
Stove spares	
Tent/personal repair kit (incl. needles, thread, material, etc.)	

Photographic & Sound Recording

Cameras	Leica Models M5, R5, R6
Film	Fuji, Blacks 100 ASA
	Ilford Pan F, FP4 XP1
Camera bags	LowePro
Video camera	Sony Sport Video 8
Micro-cassette recorders (8)	Sony
Micro-cassettes	

Environmental Science Research Equipment

Sun-photometer	University of Miami model
Snow sampling kits	Acid rain, carbon particles, pollen
Mercury sampling tubes	DSIR, New Zealand
Air pump	'Power Pump'
Thermometers	Various
Barometer	Thommon
Wind speed meter	Dwyer Instruments
Snow clean knife (PTFE)	
Aluminium case	

Appendix 5
THE STUDENT EXPEDITION
by Robert Swan

From the feedback I received when lecturing to young people about the South Pole, I knew that they cared passionately about what was happening to the planet – yet they felt remote and helpless when it came to doing anything about it. In my view they needed to be more actively involved in the care and development of their surroundings than they were just by reading text books or watching gloomy documentaries on television. I wanted to do something outrageous and truly exciting for the young to identify with.

The plan was hatched for an international group of young people to witness for themselves the impact of pollution on the supposedly unspoilt Arctic wilderness. Later, they would become ambassadors for the young of their countries, setting up a chain or network of young people to spread the environmental message. So, in April 1989, 22 students from 15 countries gathered at Eureka, Environment Canada's weather station on Ellesmere Island in the High Arctic. With no industry within a thousand miles, this ought to be one of the cleanest places on earth. Yet disturbing traces of pesticides can be found in the snow, and there is evidence, too, of acid rain, a thinning ozone layer and greenhouse gases.

Through lectures, scientific studies and outdoor activities, it was my hope that the youngsters would see for themselves the disastrous effects the world's pollution was having on the fragile Arctic.

Before arriving in the north, the student party attended a reception in Ottawa at which a clean-up programme in the Arctic was announced. Canada's north is littered with thousands of empty 45-gallon drums used for fuel caches. When later the students flew to Ellesmere Island in Twin Otters, they became the first people to participate in the programme, loading empty barrels on to the planes that always used to return empty.

The students stayed in Iqaluit in order to acclimatise to the cold and to experience life in a northern community. Each member was paired up with an Inuit student from an outlying settlement who lived in Iqaluit while attending school. For three days they had the opportunity to share in a unique culture by taking part in traditional drum dancing and throat singing.

On arrival in Eureka the student contingent outnumbered permanent residents by seven to one. They created their own environmental problem by placing excess demands on the water, sewage and garbage systems. As elsewhere, Eureka has finite resources. The water comes from a lagoon that can be filled only once a year. Food must be flown in at great expense, and garbage at the dump has very little opportunity to decay. Thus the problems that we face as a global concern were starkly illustrated at a personal level.

In Eureka the students were led by Colin Henderson through a series of challenging trust games in order to overcome cultural differences. As with much Arctic research, there was often the opportunity to combine sight-seeing with data collection. Dr Dennis Gregor came to Eureka to help the group look at the problems of acid rain in the far north. In order to see what localised effect Eureka had on the environment, they ski'd 10 km east and west of the station, taking snow samples that were later tested for conductivity (an indicator of acidity). This took the groups past some of the spectacular icebergs that had been frozen into the sound the previous autumn. Dennis had been doing research on pesticides found on the Agassiz ice-cap east of Eureka, and had detected pesticides used only in Texas!

Dr Ian Stirling, from Parks, Canada, had been studying for many years the effects of pollution on wildlife in the Arctic, where the polar bear is on top of the food chain. His studies show that these animals are full of PCBs, and that Inuit mothers' milk contains PCBs well beyond the level considered as safe.

Peter Suedfeld, the Dean of Graduate Studies at the University of British Columbia, is a psychologist who explained to the students some of the problems of living in isolated outposts in the north – and in changing peoples' behaviour with regard to the environment.

To engender an appreciation of and respect for the Arctic, the students slept in igloos, camped on the land and travelled three days by skis, pulling sleds over the frozen ice and up into the surrounding mountains. The temperatures that they encountered dropped to minus 26 degrees celsius. Wind chill added to the effect of cold.

The ultimate success of Icewalk will depend on how well the students carry the message of environment pollution to the rest of the world. This ability was shown in Eureka when the students formed a council and took responsibility for the management of their programme. Through a number of discussions and debates, a summary statement was produced that encapsulates the spirit of the student experiment.

We are commiting suicide, step by step. 'We', meaning not only the 22 young students from 15 countries who are participating in the Icewalk Arctic Expedition, but also each person living in this world.

We became aware that the world can live without us but we cannot live without the world. We are the problem, and we must be the solution. When the earth dies, we die along with it because we are part of it. So it is time to save our lives.

How? By asking ourselves, where does our energy come from? By asking ourselves where we dump our rubbish. By asking ourselves relentlessly if our actions are good for nature. By taking immediate international action together.

Because each small action can destroy or save us, each individual can make a difference.

Let's live. Let's live more simply.

Students

Tessa Blackett – New Zealand
Daniel McAvoy – Australia
Emma Westerman – Australia
Anne d'Heursel – Brazil
Pudloo Akavak – Canada
Peter Hobart – Canada
Liu Shuang – China
Gordon Mac an Bhaird – Eire (Ireland)
Roger Ho Ping Kuen – Hong Kong
Shailendra Sinha – India
Makoto Kinoshita – Japan
Stanley Mwangi Gachui – Kenya
Kate Warnock – N. Ireland
Tomomi Sakajire – Japan
Jose Leite Faria – Portugal
Irina Frolkina – USSR
Emir Adimoldaev – USSR
Michael Charlton – UK
Mike Rothbart – USA
Michael Hoyle – USA
Sonja Podein – West Germany
Andreas Hancke – West Germany

Student Escorts

Lee Scott – Canadian Student Escort
  and Expedition Logistics Officer
Lavinia Sidgwick – Co-ordinator Duke
  of Edinburgh's Award Scheme (UK)
Mandip Singh Soin – Indian Student
  Escort
Colin Henderson – British Student Escort
Wendy Wait – Australian Student Escort
Christopher Lonsdale – Hong Kong and
  Chinese Student Escort
Michihiro Shiraishi – Japanese Student
  Escort
Roland Westphal – West German
  Student Escort
Terence Davis – US Student Escort
Kirill Tchashin – USSR Student Escort
Dr Lise Loubert – Expedition Doctor

ACKNOWLEDGMENTS

Icewalk would like to express its deep appreciation to all Amway distributors and employees worldwide.

❋

It is difficult to acknowledge fully the love, support and tireless assistance given by so many since this expedition took form three long years ago, but I would like to express special gratitude to a number of people who made the wildly ambitious Icewalk dream a reality.

I thank Christopher Holloway, Lee Scott, Environment Canada, Tourism Canada, Jerry Salloum, the student escorts and the staff of the Eureka Weather Station for making the Student Expedition the wonderful success I knew it could be. I am greatly indebted to those who helped bring financial and administrative order to the expedition as it grew, including Wilfrid Grenville-Grey and Murray Fuller in the United Kingdom, Christine Gee and Grant Kearney in Australia, Kazuko Motegi in Japan, Alison Landes in New York, Christopher Lonsdale in Hong Kong, Dr Misha Malakhov in the Soviet Union and Simon Dring everywhere.

My thanks go also to those team members who made their diaries, journals and notes available in the writing of this book, especially Dr Misha Malakhov, Graeme Joy, Arved Fuchs, Darryl E. Roberts, John Tolson, Jeremy Morris and Stephen Williams; and to Rupert Summerson for the provision of maps and other valuable data. For the use of their photographs in this book I am grateful to Mike Beedell, Dr Misha Malakhov, Angus Cockney, Arved Fuchs, Hiro Onishi, Tetsuya Akiyama, *The Yomiuri Shimbun*, Roger Mear, Rebecca Ward, Ben Olds and Derek Fordham. The expedition is deeply indebted to Blacks the Photographers in Ottawa, for their generous support, and also to Leica Cameras. The Royal Institute of Navigation kindly provided maps and access to Rupert Summerson's article on polar navigation which appeared in *Navigation News*.

A special note of appreciation is due to Tracey Carpenter, Jennifer Tomas and Qantas Airways who enabled the expedition's archivist, Christine McCabe, to research and document Icewalk from its inception. Special thanks too to the intrepid pilots and ground controllers of Bradley First Air, Brent Boddy, the staff of the Ottawa General Hospital and the people of Iqaluit and Resolute Bay.

The Japanese Alpine club, the Royal Geographical Society and the Explorers Club of New York gave me invaluable advice and support, and the Duke of Edinburgh's Award Scheme generously provided patronage.

My thanks to Anthony Willoughby who ensured I was in the right place at the right time, and to Captain Giles Kershaw for always being in the right place at the right time.

I am eternally grateful for the loving support of my entire family; I know it is not easy for my mother to endure a son such as myself and I commend the courage and support of my fellow team members' families and friends.

I pay tribute to Wally Romanes, a wonderful friend and adviser, who was to have been our base camp commander had he not tragically died only months after the expedition was first planned.

Finally I thank Martyn Forrester and Christine McCabe for helping to bring order to this book, Tony Colwell for his indefatigable support as my editor at Jonathan Cape and Rowan Seymour, his very patient designer.

ROBERT SWAN

Cumbria, England
11th January, 1990

BIBLIOGRAPHY

The following books and magazine features have been quoted or consulted in the preparation of this text:

Roald Amundsen, *My Life as an Explorer*, Doubleday Doran, New York, 1927; Heinemann, London, 1927

Pierre Berton, *The Arctic Grail – The Quest for the North West Passage and the North Pole 1818–1909*, McClelland & Stewart, Toronto, 1988

Hugh Brody, *Living Arctic Hunters of the Canadian North*, Faber & Faber, London, 1987

Lester R. Brown and Alan Durning, Christopher Flavin, Lori Heise, Jodi Jacobson, Sandra Postel, Michael Renner, Cynthia Pollock Shea, Linda Starke, 'State of the World 1989' – *A Worldwatch Institute Report on Progress Toward a Sustainable Society*, S. & W. Information Guides, Melbourne, 1989

Bruce Chatwin, *The Songlines*, Jonathan Cape, London, 1987

Edward Dolan, *Matthew Henson, Black Explorer*, Dodd, Mead & Co., New York, 1979

Ranulph Fiennes, *To the Ends of the Earth – Transglobe Expedition 1979–82*, Hodder & Stoughton, London, 1983

Martyn Forrester, *The Survival Skills Handbook*, Sphere Books, London, 1988

Wally Herbert, *The Noose of Laurels*, Hodder & Stoughton, London, 1989

Wally Herbert, *The North Pole*, Sackett & Marshall, London, 1979

Barry Lopez, *Arctic Dreams*, Scribner's, New York, 1986

Roger Mear and Robert Swan, *In the Footsteps of Scott*, Jonathan Cape, London, 1987

A. A. Milne, *Winnie-the-Pooh*, Methuen, London, 1926

Fridtjof Nansen, *Farthest North* (2 volumes), Harper, New York, 1897; Newnes, London, 1898

Robert E. Peary, 'Discovery of the Pole: Peary's First Account', *World's Work*, October 1909

—— , *The North Pole*, Hodder & Stoughton, London, 1910

Captain R. F. Scott, *Scott's Last Expedition*, Smith, Elder & Co., London, 1913

Vilhjalmur Stefansson, *Great Adventures & Expeditions*, Dial, New York, 1952

Will Steger with Paul Schurke, *North to the Pole*, Times Books, New York, 1987

James A. Wilkerson, MD (Editor), Cameron C. Bangs, MD, John S. Hayward, Ph.D., *Hypothermia, Frostbite and other Cold Injuries*, The Mountaineers, Seattle Washington, 1986

SPONSORS AND SUPPORTERS
PRIMARY SPONSOR: AMWAY JAPAN LTD

AUSTRALIA

Sponsors
AGC Finance
Brian Alderson
Amatil Limited
Anchor Australia
Ansett Airlines
Apple Computers
Arnotts Biscuits
Australian
   Geographic
   Magazine
Australian Life
   Products
Bank of New Zealand
Behrens Browne
Bill Bass Optical
Black & Decker
Mike Boland
Bondi Olympic Gym
Cadbury
   Confectionery
Canadian Airlines
Champion
   Photographs
The Chart Room
Continental Australia
Craddock, Murray &
   Neumann
Damart Thermolactyl
Dow Corning
   Australia
Downs & Son
Duracell Batteries
Dwyer Instruments
Dr Bill George
Garry Gleeson
Captain John Hall
Harry M. Miller's
   Speakers' Bureau
Hatton Seiko

Herald and Weekly
   Times
Hewlett-Packard
High Tops
   Equipment
Honeywell Bull
   Computers
Infomagic Australia
Interaction Associates
Jobsons Year Book
Kingtread Ltd
Richards McCallum
The Macquarie Bank
Macson Trading
Meiko Cases
Microsoft Ltd
Lynton & Joanne
   Morris
Mountain Designs
Sonny Naidu
National Panasonic
Nova Graphics
Ogilvy & Mather
John Oliff
Omnicom
Penta Group
Photovision
   Melbourne
Qantas Airways
Rezal Industries
Robbi Newman
   Photography
Rosella Lipton
Saft Batteries
Sanitarium Health
   Food Co.
Scott Cameron
   Photography
Sunvalley True Fruits
Sydney Allen Printers
Sydney Motorcycle
   Wreckers

Toyota Motor Sales
Tullett & Tokyo
T. W. Sands & Co
Videoplus Ltd
Wang Australia
Westfield
   Management
Wilderness
   Equipment
W. L. Gore & Assoc.
World Expeditions

Supporters
Hugh Anderson
Tony & Lucy Axford
Frank Bartlett
Yasmin Boland
Ken Boys
Bronwyn Bronz
Margot Buttrose
Melissa Coghlan
Riccardo Coombes &
   Tina
Liz Courtney
Crash Craddock
Michael Culkin
Gordon Davis
Tom Dery
David & Jane
   Fanshawe
Bill Ferris
Dr Bruce Forgan
Warwick Foy
Peter Freudenstein
Christine Gee
Margaret Gee
Dr Graeme Goldin
Peter Hertzstein
John Hopkins
David Iggulden
Robert Johnston
Alan Jones

Greg Jones
Bonnie Mary Joy
Donna Joy
Grant Kearney
Nick Kostos
John & Val McCabe
Ian McMahon
Peter Malcolm
Joe & Sally Manning
Cathy Martin
Harry M. Miller
David Mooney
Margaret Moore
Tracey Morgan
Goronwy Price
Nima Price
Jenny Reid
Dale Rhodes
Mish Rowe
Phil Scanlen
Charles Shipley
Dick Smith
Graham South
Janet Summerson
Victoria Taylor
Katherine Vogel
John Walton
Victoria Weir
Mark Williams
Richard Wylie

BRAZIL

Sponsors and Supporters
Casa Faro Tourismo
Simon & Marcia
   Clayton
Globo Radio and
   Television
R. V. A. Industria
St Paul's School (São
   Paulo)

CANADA

Sponsors
Acuvue Contact
  Lenses
Adventure Canada
Adventure Network
  (Vancouver)
Alexander Battery
Agonquin Travel
Anderson, Smythe &
  Kelly
Andre Moreau
  Gastronomie
Apace Screen
  Printing
Apple Canada
Baffin Regional
  Health Board
Barry Cordage
Blacks Photo Corp.
Bradley First Air
Brisson Pharmacy
Canada Poste
Canadian Airlines
Canadian Airlines
  International
  (Toronto)
Canadian Imperial
  Bank of Commerce
Canadian Museums
  Corp.
Canadian Parks
  Services
Canadian Thermos
Carleton Recreational
  Equipment
Chromascan (Ottawa)
Coast Mountain
  Sports (Vancouver)
Conexus Research
  Group
CTV
Daymen Photo
  Marketing
Do-Gree Fashions
Environment Canada
Exel Limited
External Affairs
  Canada
Fletcher Leisure
  Group
Fredal's Office
  Equipment
Gausthaus
  Switzerland
Government of North
  West Territories
Hanson Mohawk
Harvest Food Works

Helly Hansen
Hudson Inc.
Igloo Vikski Inc.
Inuit Broadcasting
  Corp.
Iqaluit Hospital
Irving Rivers
Johnson Diversified
Kanuk
Kaufman Footwear
Laidlaw Transit Rd
Loblaws (Toronto)
Maryvon Dairy
  Products
Matsushita Electric of
  Canada
Mexicali Rosas
Narwhal Inn
  (Resolute Bay)
Navigator Inn
  (Iqaluit)
Nicholas International
  Hostel (Ottawa)
Nikon Canada
Norca Industries
Office of the Prime
  Minister of Canada
OOC Travel
Ottawa Hospital
Otto's Service Centre
Paris Gloves
Peacebridge
Peepers (Ontario)
Plastic Contact Lens
  Company
Polaroid Canada
Polyfab
Procem Photo Prods
Revenue Canada
Runge Press (Ottawa)
Smico Canada
Sony of Canada
Steenberg
  Construction
  (Iqaluit)
Swix Ski Sticks
Taymor Industries
Telesat Canada
Tourism Canada
Trailhead
Transport Canada
  (Iqaluit)
Ukavik Student
  Residence (Iqaluit)
Western Fibres
Zippy Print

Supporters
Dave Akeeagok
Brian Allard

Fred Alt
Angela (Ottawa)
Peter Baird
Mike Balshaw
Mike Beedell
Michel A. Bilodeau
Yvon Blanchete
Peter Brebner
Brent Boddy
Dr Jocelyne
  Bourgeois
Leslie Buchanan
Sharon Buness
Douglas Cardinal
Leo Carriere
Dr John Catching
Trish Cockney
Hugh Culver
Doug Currie
Jackie Czernin
Mike Daoust
Eddy Decouto
Dora Delmish
Tony Deveau
Wayne Edmond
Fast Eddy
Dave Freeze
Barry Garrett
Maureen Garrity
David Gilday
John Goodwin
Tod Gorr
Dr Dennis Gregor
Linda Gun
Susan Hamlin
Dean Hammill
Edna Hofer
Pia Holloway
Ralph Horne
The Inuit People of
  the Circum Polar
  Region
John Jamieson
Bezal & Terry
  Jesudason
Bruce Jonasson
Jonny (Iqaluit)
Rolf Jors
Rudi Keller
Kavavow Kiguktak
Dr Roy Koerner
Paul Larocque
Igor Lobanov
Douglas Longmeyer
Donna MacGarvie
Ken McKury
Alan Mclean
Peter Martin
Brian Menton
John Merritt

Maurice Nau
Laurie Nowakowski
Curt Petrovich
Kelly Phaneuf
Trevor Pollitt
Louis Poulin
Jerry Salloum
Bonnie Jean
  Sandiford
Wally Schaber
Joe Setter
Peter Snedfeld
Greg Stansfield
Keith Staples
Jens Steenberg
Cathy Stevenson
Dr Ian Stirling
Dennis Stossel
Monique Sutherland
Pit Taylor
James Thompson
Bill Thorpe
Jennifer Tomas
Dr Neil Trivett
Hans Weber
Richard Weber
Gareth Wood
Andy Yun

FRANCE

Sponsors
AGC Finance
Compagnie General
  Horiogere
Damart
  Thermolactyl

HONG KONG

Sponsors
Burson-Marsteller
  Ltd
Ogilvy & Mather

Supporters
Roger G. Hum
Giles & Anne
  Kershaw
Chris Lonsdale
Maggie McBride
Douglas Maran
Peter Rawlston

INDIA

Sponsors
Air India

British Aerospace
Ibex Equipment
Ibex Expeditions
Tata Iron & Steel
  Company

Supporters
Mandip Singh Soin

JAPAN

Sponsors
Asics Corporation
Damart Thermolactyl
Dentsu PR
Dunlop Leisure
  Sports
Foreign
  Correspondents
  Club of Japan
Fuji Photo Film
Japanese Alpine Club
Japan Times
Liebermann Co.
Mont-Bell Co.
New Takanawa
  Prince Hotel
Shingo Nomura (One
  World Fund)
Sony Corporation
Swan Lense
Tullett & Tokyo
Yomiuri Shimbun
Yomiuri Shimbun
  Junior Press

Supporters
Tetsuya Akiyama
Thomas E. Doyle
Bill & Magee
  Hemmer
Tsuguyasu Itami
Itsuki Iwata
Mike Jacobs
Yosoji Kobayashi
Kenya Mizukami
Kazuko Motegi
Shiyeyuki Okajima
Toshiaki Onishi
Lidia Renyi
Karen Rose
Kuniomi Sakai
Michihiro Shiraishi
Hiroyuki Suzuki
Motokichiro Ushiki
Anthony & Victoria
  Willoughby
Ko Yoshida

KENYA

Sponsors and supporters
Barclays Bank
Starehe Boys School
  (Nairobi)
Alan Tivey

NEW ZEALAND

Sponsors
Alliance Freeze Dried
  Foods
Arthur Ellis & Co.
Breadcraft
Damart Thermolactyl
Fairydown Outdoors
Featherstone County
  Council
Kodak N.Z.
Lake Ferry Hotel
Masterton Lands
  Trust
N.Z. Dairy Board
Venturetreks

Supporters
Mr & Mrs C.V. Bargh
Mr Burns
Dr Chad Dick
Mr & Mrs J. Hume
Mr & Mrs W. Hume
Mr & Mrs D.
  McIlraith
Mr & Mrs S. Ogilvie
Pirinoa School
Mr & Mrs J. Stephen
Mrs E. M. Thomas

PORTUGAL

Sponsors
FNAC
Instituto Da
  Juventude
Jornal de Noticia
Jose Faria
Mundial Confianca
Robbialac Portuguesa
Shell Portuguesa
TAP (Air Portugal)
Teixeira Duarte

Supporters
Teresa Oliveira Dias
Frederico Martins
  Mendes
Alfredo Marques

Jose Mario
Maria Eugenia Inacio
Jorge Fernandes

UNITED KINGDOM
& EIRE

Sponsors
Agfa-Gevaert (Dublin)
Apple UK
Bain & Co.
Barclays Bank
Berghaus
Bord Bainne (Dublin)
Cameron Hall
Cargo Development
  Company
Casella
Mike Chantrey
Mr Charlton
Citroen (Bradford)
Clydesdale Bank
Coombes Wales
  Quinnell
Co. Kildare
  Vocational Educa-
  tion Committee
Dalgety Agriculture
Damart Thermolactyl
David Shepherd
  Charitable
  Foundation
Tom Docherty
Electricity Supply
  (Dublin)
Farnham Herald
F. K. I.
  Communications
Foton
Great Outdoors
  (Dublin)
Hartlepool Lotteries
Helly Hansen UK
Hilltrekker
Interaction Assoc.
Jack Wolfskin (N.
  Ireland)
Jack Wolfskin
  (Penrith)
J. W. Cameron & Co.
Karrimor
  International
Leica Cameras UK
Lloyds Bank
Mercury
  Communications
Mount Everest
  Foundation

National Westminster
  Bank
Northern Echo
P. A. Liddle & Sons
Marilyn Potts
The President's
  Award (Republic of
  Ireland)
Tom Raine
Sherwoods of
  Darlington
Slattery's Camera
  Circle (Dublin)
Slip Inn (Barras)
Alan Smith
Snow-Sled
Special Forces Club
Students' Union,
  Stranmillis College
Swinton Insurance
Teesdale Council
Thomas Miller
  Insurance
Tindle Newspapers
Trimedia
  Communications
T. Smith & Sons
Tullett & Tokyo
Tyne Tees TV
West Hartlepool
  Steam Navigation
  Company
C. B. Williams &
  James
YMCA Herrington
  Burn

Supporters
Gillian Acres
Sheila Acres
Nick Barr
Jacky Billington
Bert Bissell
Ian Blenkinsop
Chris Bolsover
Line Boyer
Robin & Lindy
  Brockway
Simon Brookes-Ward
Patrick Campbell
Nick Cater
Mr & Mrs C. Cavan
Mike Chantry
Jane Chia
Peter Christopherson
Colin Clarke
Ian Coombes
Anne Cooper
Mike Corby
Brig. P. Cordingley

Geoff Cox
Simon Cummins
Roger Dayne
Ben and Samuel the
  Dogs
John Donner
Richard Down
Emma Drake
John & Rebecca Drew
Simon Dring
Peter Eaves
Kit Elliott
Michael Farmer
Sir Ranulph Fiennes
Mark Fox-Andrews
John Friend
Sir Vivian Fuchs
Murray Fuller
Ray Funnell
Sir Geoffrey
  Gilbertson
Dr Michael Gormley
Wilfrid Grenville-
  Grey
Margaret Groves
Jonathan & Julia Hart
Wally Herbert
Alan Higbey
Michael Holmes
Eleanor Honnywill
Jane Howe
Flo & Morag Howell
Christopher Howes
Tessa Howes
Peter Huck
Lord Hunt
M. Jebb
Anne Johnson
Dave Jones
Chris Jones
David Keene
Steve & Wendy
  Keith-Roach
Clive Kerfoot
Dan Laurie
Joe Lee
Clara Legge-Bourke
Paul Leigh
Charlie McKelvie
James Mackewan
Chris & Karen Main
David Major
Michael Marmion
Peter Marsden
Nigel Metcalfe
John Norris
Peter Moulson
Simon Normanton
Richard Olivier
Mr and Mrs J. O'Neill

Gordon Owen
Vicram & Joanna
  Pardy
John Park
Mike Parsons
Janie Patterson
Sir Gerard Peat
Cassandra Phillips
Don & Pat Pratt
Annie Price
Samantha Pullen
Robin Radley
David Read
Stella Rooke
Donald & Jill
  Rushbrooke
Jill Rushbrooke
Lucinda Rykens
Michael Sangar Davis
  and Family
Domonic & Mary
  Sasse
Sir Peter Scott
Lord Shackleton
Lady Sharples
Mike Shepherd
Peter & Lavinia
  Sidgwick
Sir George Sinclair
Denis Stone
Dr Michael Stroud
Hugo Summerson
Michael Swaddling
Douglas Swan
Margaret Swan
Thomas Swan
Thelma Tetaur
Mr D. Thompson
Ray Tindle
Sally Tolson
Hedley Trigge
Derek Tullett
Jonny Usher
David & Susan Vigar
Mr & Mrs J. M.
  Warnock
Miss N. Warnock
Richard White
World Fellowship
Claire Worlidge
David Wynne-
  Williams

*The Duke of Edinburgh's
  Award Scheme*
James Brown (N.Z.)
Com. David Cobb
  (Australia)
James Foster (Kenya)

Colin Henderson
  (N. Ireland)
Major-Gen. M. Hobbs
Marilyn Lewis
John Murphy (Eire)
Com. David Newing
Eric Rainey
  (N. Ireland)
Andy Reade
Marion Samworth
  (Canada)
Maria Ting (H.K.)
Eric Worrall

UNITED STATES

Sponsors
Aladdin Industries
Aladdin International
Alpine Research
America M Bank
Amway Audio Visual
Amway Grand Plaza
  Hotel
Amway PR (Michigan)
Apple Computers
Booth Newspapers
Bushwacker
  Backpacker
Carr, Goodson & Lee
Cascade Designs
Coleman Co.
Damart Thermolactyl
Explorers' Club
Fort Worth Star
  Telegraph
Grabber
  Handwarmers
Harvard Business
  School
Institute of Resource
  Management
Kenko International
Landstar Productions
Latham & Watkins
Library of Congress
Life Link
  International
Marriott Hotels
Masters of the Arctic
  Exhibit
Mountain Safety
  Research
Nalge (Special
  Products)
Nutrilite
PBS
Proserve (Texas)

Sherpa (Chicago)
Smith & Joyce
Surefoot Corp.
Thermapac
Tigon Corp.
Uniset Inc.
United Nations
  Environment
  Programme
White Rock Athletic
  Club

Supporters
Dr Darrick Antell
Robert Beltic
Steve Bernard
Brad & Anne Bishop
Denny Bowman
Dr Noel Brown
John Bruno
Bill Bruyere
Kim Bruyn
Jessica Church
Dr Tony Clarke
Joe Corella
Martine Coursil
Darlene Cress
Jim Daniel
De Vos family
Kathy Didion
Dr Dunn
Jean Claude Faby
Douglas Fieldhouse
John Germain
Ned Gillette
Debbie Graff
David Hancock
Tad Heitmann
Robert Hoffman
G. Dulany Howland
Sophia Ibrahim
Chuck & Suzy Jacobs
Hasty Johnson
Sandy Klim
Dan Klores
Alison Landes
Norma Lee
John Levinson
Robert & Susan
  Lynch
Donna Matrazzo
Pam Mettler
Len Meyer
Terry Minger
Jane Neilson
Sandi Nicholson
Nigel Nobel
Ben Olds
Ross Perot

Ross Perot Junior
Paul Ramer
Robert Redford
Leigh Anne Reynolds
Howard Rubenstein
Satori School
Bruce Savin
Mort & Jane Scott
Randy Schroeder
Saundra Shoen
Michael Smith
Keith Staples
Gary Sumihiro
Lida Anne Thomas
Dr Mostafa Tolba
Alexie Torres
Charles & Sharon
  Usher
Van Andel family
Sally Van Slooten
Eleanor Vierheilig
Rebecca Ward
Elizabeth Williams
John Williams

USSR

Sponsors
Biryulevo
  Experimental
  Factory
Gosstrakh
Institute of
  Biomedical
  Problems
Luxury Fashion
  Centre
Medical Workers
  Trade Union
Ministry of Health
Pravda Newspaper
Rjazan Youth Science
  Technique Centre
Rjazan Machine-
  Tools
Rjazan Youth Group
Rodniki Fur Factory
RSFSR (Red Cross)
Russian Medical Inst.

Science Research
  Institute of Honey
Society for Protection
  of Environment
Soviet Culture Fund
Sovietski Sport News
Sputnik Youth Travel
State Institute of
  Drugs' Standard-
  isation
Union of
  Co-operatives of
  Alma-Ata Region

Supporters
Alla
Roy Dallison
Lazo Kovacevic
Leav
Olga Malakhov
Prof. Mikhail Novikov
Prof. Evgeny Stroev
Kirill Tchashin
Prof. R. Tigranyan

Swan & Co., Moscow
Yuri

WEST GERMANY

Sponsors
Ajungilak
Climb High
C. Plath
Hamburg-Munchener
  Ersatzkasse
Horzu
Karrimore Germany
Leica GmbH
Procem Photo
  Production
Schwarzkopf GmbH

Supporters
Heather Digby
Brigitte Ellerbrock
Prof. Dieter Otten
Klaus Gunter Peter

INDEX

Figures in italic indicate plate numbers

Aconcagua mountain (Argentina) 174
advance base camp, *see* Columbia, Cape
air drops 132, 156; *see also* resupply
airstrips 129, 132; problems of 189
Akiyama-san 67–8
Alert Weather Station 78
Amatil reconnaissance 25, 62
Amundsen, Roald 53, 64, 133
Amway, Japan, as sponsors
  29–30, 212
animal skin, as protection against cold 86
Anne, student 149
Antarctic expeditions, criticism of 13
Antarctic Treaty, renegotiation (1991)
  18
Antarctica 18, 53; Christmas Day in 145;
  environmental damage 18; *see also*
  Footsteps of Scott expedition
Apple Macintosh computers 50–1
Arctic Ocean 31, 34, 162, *15*; distances
  in 73; magic of 133; pollution 93–5;
  survival, water problems 102–4; vision
  in 73
Arctic exploration: history of 133–6;
  international co-operation in 136
Arctic Grail, The (Berton), 53
Argos Satellite tracking service 51;
  beacons 143, 197
arguments 82, 125–6, 176–7; non-
  divisive 157–60
arrival date 118, 129, 132, 161, 206,
  208–9
atmosphere, ionospheric disturbances 62,
  84
Australia, HQ in 22–3
Australian Geographic 17

backpacks 107, 112, 115, *21*
Baffin Island, North West Territories 28
Barclays Bank 16

Base Camp, *see* Columbia; Resolute
Beardmore Glacier, Antarctica *5*
bears, fear of 139, 196, *58*
Beaufort Island, Antarctica 13
Beedall, Mike 78
Belfast: CFC recycling plant 150; student
  from 150
Bering, Vitus 133
Bleathgill, Cumbria 201
Blenkinsop, Ian 98
blisters 11, 89–90, 101, 104, 116, 125,
  145–6, 155
Boddy, Brent 34, 39
Booth Newspaper Group, Michigan 150
boots: chewing into shape 51; frozen 106,
  112; as pillow 83
Bradley Air 55, 132, 146, *77*; floating fuel
  cache 198
Bradshaw & Webb, Mercedes dealers 15
bridges 142, 167, 171, *93, 98, 118*
British Antarctic Survey 18
Brody, Hugh 34–5
Broni, Steve 15, 16, 17–18
buckwheat, inedible 125–6
Bush, President George 63

Cabot, Sebastian 133
Canada, Inuit integration
  programmes 182
Castle Brough 201
Cathay, NW Passage to 133
Charles, Prince of Wales 63
Chatwin, Bruce 137
Chernobyl nuclear power plant explosion
  95
Cherry-Garrard, Apsley 136
Chinborazo mountain (Ecuador) 174
Chopikarki mountain 174
Cockney, Angus Kaanerk (Gus) 28, 42,
  72, 82, 83, 91, 112, 127, 142, 164, *14,*

Cockney, Angus Kaanerk (Gus) (*cont*.):
  26, 27, as champion skier 28, 74–5,
  91, 100; in front 84, 116–17, 137, 140,
  145, 156; homesickness 117, 182, 209;
  as leader 201; role 72, 74–5, 154, 157
cold: clothing, appropriate 78–9, 86–7,
  112; hazards of 87, 101; survival in 45,
  72,78, 86–8, 102–4; and wind 86
Columbia, Cape, advance base camp 11,
  34, 51, 118, *6, 34, 35, 36*; arrival at
  61–72; departure for 53; leaving 73;
  radio blackout 143, 156; radio contact
  with 102, 168, 186, 189; Resolute, link
  56; team 62
continental shelf 88
co-operation, international 82, 129, 137
cracked hands 155, 176

Danny, student 149
'Dark Horse' (stove) 154
Dave, sound man 106
Day, Crispin 62, 67, 77, 78, 189
De Vos, Rich 29–30
dehydration 102–3
diaries 117, *60, 75*
Discovery, relic of 171, 189, 201
Down, Richard 29
Drake, Emma 162, 171
dress 78–9, 86–7, 112
drifting ice 88, 127, 152, 154, 200, 201
Duke of Edinburgh's Award Scheme 34,
  149
Durham, schooldays 21
Durham University 133

Edinburgh, Prince Philip, Duke of 16
85th parallel 50, 146
84th parallel 117, 123
89th parallel 195
87th parallel 187, 188
86th parallel 168
Ellesmere Island 73, *33*
Emma, student 149
environmental damage: Antarctica 18;
  Arctic 93–5; youth and 19
equipment: transporting 66; weight of 59,
  66
Eskimos, *see* Inuit people
Etienne, Jean Louis 53
Eureka, Canadian Arctic Weather Station
  57–9, 178–9, *32*; bad weather 198;
  last comforts in 58–9; low visibility
  130; resupply from 12, 34; student
  expedition in 92, 107
Evans, Cape 12, 18, 21
Evans, Edgar 201
Everest, Hiro climbs 209

exhaustion *107*; self-perpetuating 193–4;
  threshold 95, 145; and vagueness 187
exploration: defined 136–7; value of 189
explorers: early 133–6; qualities needed
  37

Farman, Joseph 18
Fiennes, Sir Ranulph 16, 57, 61, 64; base
  camp 64, 68; large sledges 53, 64
Fine Young Cannibals 164
fires, tent 39, 85, 107
Flowers, Pam, expedition 61, 122, 168
fog 127–8
food 39, 78, 86, 92–3, 128, 164, *49, 95*;
  rations 132; shortage 127, 130
Footsteps of Scott expedition (1985)
  12–18, 61; funding 15–18, 21; as
  learning ground 157; setbacks 13–14,
  98, 208; simplicity of 69
Franklin, Sir John 78, 87, 133
Frobisher Bay, training trip in 28, 34–56
Frobisher, Sir Martin 133
frostbite 42–8, 56, 162–3; in blacks 25,
  64; metal in 87; in ravens 49; universal
  116
Fuchs, Arved 11, 25–7, 55, 72, 89, 116,
  128, 130, 137, 164, 171, 176, 182, 195,
  214, *11, 27, 63, 79*; frostbite 42, 116,
  155, 193; health 11, 67, 113, 115, 116,
  118, 155
fuel: problems 142; resupply 98, 101,
  105–7; shortage 11, 76–7, 93, 101,
  130
fur, as defence against cold 86

Gachui, Stanley 149
Gee, Christine 23
German Scientific Association 136
Gandhi, Prime Minister Ranjiv 63
good luck charms 56, 171, 201
Grand Rapids (Mich.) Amway HQ 29
Greenpeace 18

Hall, Charles Francis 136
Hammer, Bill 29
Hargreaves, Jim 34, 106
Hawke, Prime Minister 63
Hayward, Sir Jack 22, 162
health problems 67, 89–90, 116–18
heat, life without 104–5; *see also* cold
Helly Hansen suits 112
Henderson, Colin 149, 150
Henson, Matthew 24, 64, *10*
Herbert, Wally 189
Holloway, Christopher 34, 162
Hong Kong, environmental awareness
  exhibitions 150

Huaskaran mountain 174
Hudson, Henry 133
Hughes Janet 24
Hutchison, Kirstie 15, 34
hygiene programme 136

ice: change in character 123; depth of,
    138, 142; moving 127, 152, 154, 200,
    201; ridges 152, 45, rubble 156, 81,
    special performance 178; thin 152–4,
    182
Iceland, Vatnajokull icecap 21
Ice Station, Soviet 118, 132, 189–91,
    196
Icewalk expedition: absurdity of 188; am-
    bitions 160; arrival date 118, 129, 132,
    161, 206, 208–9; bridge building 150;
    disorganisation 35, 73–4, 109; evacu-
    ation 213–14; failure, fear of 69; 'finds
    itself' 142, 157–60; funding 25, 27,
    29–30, 53; HQ 22; international team
    19, 26, 27, 31, 38, 92, 109, 129;
    language barriers 38, 88, 128, 143,
    160, 169, 178–9; last push 200–6;
    leadership 37–8, 48; media attention
    to 39, 42, 48, 66, 199, 209, 214–15,
    216; members as animals 195–6; at
    North Pole 206, 208–9;origins 12, 18;
    predictions about 162; preparations
    31–4, 37–59; press conference 214,
    125; as race 92, 138, 144, 162, 163,
    169, 196; records 182; recruitment for
    21–8; research role 55, 55–7, 107,
    109, 115, 162–3, 190; setting out
    59–73; slower members, removal 56,
    91, 115, 117, 145, 160, 162, 169, 181;
    student expedition 19, 92, 146; team
    spirit 38, 48, 54, 69, 91–2, 116–17;
    urgency, sense of 123
illness, problems with 67, 116–18,
    189–90
In Pisco mountain 174
In the Footsteps of Scott 18; *see also* Foot-
    steps of Scott expedition
injury, risk of 200
insoles, importance of, 145–6
Interaction Associates 29
international co-operation 82, 109, 129,
    137
International Polar Year, First (1882) 136
International Public Speakers Con-
    ference, Washington DC 28
Inuit people 28, 34–5; Canadian integra-
    tion programme 182; dress 79, 86–7;
    survival and travel methods 53; sweat
    113
Inuvik (Mackenzie Delta) 182

ionospheric disturbances 62, 84
Iqaluit, training trip in 28, 34–56, 16, 17,
    20,22, 29, 30
Ishikawa, Yoshi 62
isolation, value of 189
Iwata-san 67–8

Japan, Ministry of the Environment 63
Japanese Alpine Club 27
John Biscoe, RRS 21
Johnny, Inuit carpenter 55
Joy, Graeme 23, 24, 38, 42, 55, 67, 72,
    79, 100, 107, 113–14, 142, 156, 157,
    164, 167–8, 189, 195, 214, 8, 26, 27,
    38, 70, 103; exhaustion 95, 167–8,
    193; experience 45; in front 84,
    116–17, 137, 140, 156, 164; health 67,
    89, 95, 101, 104, 155, 176; impatience
    91–2, 115, 116–17, 145, 169; as
    leader 38, 166, 201; as radio operator
    12, 88, 104, 143, 180, 190, 198, 59

kamik boots 28; chewing into shape 51;
    frozen 106, 112; as pillow 83
Karrimor packs 112
Kennedy, Senator Edward 28
Kershaw, Capt. Giles 17, 212
Kirill, Soviet student escort 179, 190, 191

landing strips 129, 132, 189
language problems 38, 88, 128, 143, 160,
    169, 178–9
leadership 37–8, 48
leads of water, open 89, 128, 132, 140,
    142, 151, 156, 72, 73, 90, 97, 98, 104
Lonsdale, Chris 150
Lovejoy, Tim 15, 16, 17–18

Mako Expedition 61, 122, 161, 168, 179,
    195
Makoto, student, 150
Malakhov, Mikhail (Misha) 11, 27, 35,
    38, 42, 48, 49, 51–3, 77, 82, 85, 95,
    100, 113, 125,129, 137, 142, 155, 160,
    164, 190–1, 196, 214, 12, 27, 46, 75,
    93, 124; determination 52, 59, 82, 93,
    145, 176; dogmatism 37, 38, 48, 51–3,
    78, 176–7; as expedition doctor 42–4,
    48, 66–7, 68, 89–90, 98, 108–9, 136,
    145, 155, 164, 175–6, 181, 62; experi-
    ence 37, 48–9, 72, 82; as leader 37,
    39, 48, 74–5, 82, 84, 126, 128, 138,
    156–7, 163, 169, 200, 201; personality
    176–7; praise from 171
marching 87–8, 65; night 191–2;
    records 176, 181

Mear, Roger 12, 14, 15, 21, 26, 82, 98;
  as navigator 209; as team member
  157
Messner, Reinhold 26
Michael, student, 150
migratory species, aggressiveness 137–8
Mike, photographer 106
Mike, student 149
milk rations 125
morale, low 99, 101
morning routines 112–13
Morris, Jeremy 50–1, 56–7, 68, 143,
  176, 190, 198, 31
Mulroney, Prime Minister 63

Nansen, Fridtjof 133
Nicholson, Bill 30, 213
night marching 191–2
Nomura, Shingo 27, 66
Norca sledges 112
North Pole arrival at 118, 129, 132, 161,
  206, 208–9, 120; challenge of 135–6;
  flags raised at 213; international co-
  operation in 136; race to 92, 138, 144,
  162, 163, 169, 196; Soviet ice station
  118, 132, 161, 189–91, 196; TV live
  from 118, 162
North West Passage, search for 133
Northern Ireland 149–50
Nutrilite company 30

oceans, frozen 89
Okajima-san 27
Onishi, Hiro 27, 38, 39, 42, 55–6, 72,
  88, 92, 100, 104, 112–13, 116, 128,
  143, 160, 164, 178, 201, 214, 13, 27,
  43, 60, 66, 96; climbing skills 84, 122,
  174; as cook 88, 92; exhaustion 142,
  143, 163, 176, 193, 201, 209; eye
  damage 186; humour 88, 128, 175;
  isolation 172–4; personality 172–5;
  slowness 84, 144–5, 162, 166, 176;
  team spirit 56
open leads 89, 128, 150, 142, 151, 156,
  73, 90, 97, 98, 104
open water 162, 176, 200, 72, 109;
  crossing 169–71; as danger signal 123,
  128
orange juice, frozen 199
Ottawa 31, 34, 78, 161; press conference
  216; student expedition 146; supply
  line from 34
ozone layer, measuring 18, 68, 78, 40, 87
ozonesondes 68, 78, 40

pack ice, drifting 200, 201
pain threshold 95, 145

pastimes 164
Peary, Robert E. 18, 133, 160, 213, 10;
  frostbite 89; funding 29; signpost 64,
  37
pemmican 39, 86, 92, 164
personality changes under stress 126, 128
Peter, student 149
Peter the Great, Emperor of Russia 133
Phippen, Graham 15
pilots, skill 198–9
polar bears 100, 58
Polar Bridge expedition 39, 82, 162
Polar Haven, Cape Columbia 50, 62–3,
  66, 69, 180, 35, 39
pollution: Antarctica 18; Arctic 93–5
position, fixing, 140
Pratt, Don 16
pressure ridges 42, 73, 83, 119, 163, 45,
  54; colours 93; omnipresent 154; problems of 183–6
Price, Annie 15
Punta Arenas, Chile 17
Pytheas, explorer 133

radio transmission 12, 42, 180, 190;
  problems with 11, 12, 62–3, 88, 102,
  143, 156, 196, 197, 198
Rainey, Eric 149
rashes, avoidance 136
rations, quantities 132, 17, 76
ravens 49–50; frostbite 49
Redford Institute for Resource Management 29
Redford, Robert 29
Rehnberg, Sam 30
Raynaud's phenomenon 46
Resolute Base Camp 34, 50–1, 68, 78:
  bad weather 130, 198; Cape Columbia
  link 56; differences of opinion with
  190–1; press conference 199, 200,
  209, 214–15; radio blackout 156; radio
  contact with 190–1; refuelling in
  56–7; stores 56; storms 130
rest days 132–9
resupply 12, 56, 102, 105–7, 129, 130,
  161, 186, 76, 94; air drops 132, 156;
  arguments over 176–7; delayed 127,
  129–30; difficulties of 198–9; shopping list 180
ridges, ice 152; see also pressure ridges
'river', crossing 166–7
Rjazan Machine Tool Manufacturing
  Amalgamation 49
Rjazan village 128
Roberts, Darryl E. 25, 156, 164, 171,
  214, 9, 26, 27; blistered heel 11, 90,
  101, 104, 116, 125, 145–6, 155, 176,

181, 194–5, *52, 85*; frostbite 11, 25, 42–8, 68, 77, *193, 23, 24, 25*; inexperience 92; slow progress 145, 163; withdrawal, possible 44, 46, 48, 68, 72, 90, 106–7, 160–2, 176
Ross Island, Antarctica 12
Ross, Sir James 31, 133
Royal Geographical Society 16, 22

safety, as first priority 26
Sassella, Dean 62, 63
sastrugi 79, 83
Scott, Lee 34
Scott, Robert Falcon 171; death 104, 109; fuel shortage 11; South Pole route 21
sea ice, drifting 88, 127, 152, 154, 200, 201
Sedbergh, school 16
Sentinel 164
sextant readings 140
Shackleton, Sir Ernest 18
Shailendra, student 149
shear zone 88, *52*
Shelley, Mary 78
Sidgwick, Lavinia 34
ski sticks broken 164, 171
ski-bindings broken 99, 128
skiing styles 100
skin rashes, avoidance 136
skis: length 48, 51–2; missing 166–7
sledges 39, 42; amphibious 162, *18*; large 42, 52–3, 55, 75, 107, 154, *92, 106*; as repositories 188, 201; sleeping in 95–8; small 113, *21;* weight 66
sleeping bags, frozen 85, 104, 107, 112, 128
'sleeping system' 164
Smith, Dick 17, 212
snowmobiles, cost 39
snow: samples 107; soft 64, *57, 66*
South Pole expedition (1985) 12–18, 21, 98; arrival at Pole 13–14, 98; financial problems of 14–16, 21; as learning ground 157; predictions about 162; setbacks 13–14, 98, 208; simplicity of 69
Southern Quest, sinking of 13, 15, 98, 208, *2*
Soviet expedition, 61, 168, 197
Soviet Ice Station 118, 132; abandoned 189–91, 196, *111, 112*
Soviet stoves 38, 39, 48, 77, 85–6, 107, 109, 204; problems with 199
Soviet Union: sponsorship 49; and West Germany 129
sponsorship 25, 27, 29–30, 34, 49

spring melt *117*
Stanwyck, Keith 62
Starehe Boys Centre 149
Steenberg, Jens 55
Steger, Will 63, 93–5
storms 129–30, 142–3, 151–2
stoves: difficulties of 11, 142, 154, 199; lighting *83*; Soviet 38, 39, 48, 77, 85–6, 107, 109, 204
Stroud, Mike 61
student expedition *87, 105*; arrival at Iqaluit 168; bridge building through 92, 150, *89*; depart for home 199; effort involved 146–8; Eureka, arrives at 107, 176, 179; first contact with 179–80; importance 146; involvement 19; leader 34; preparations 146–50; setting out 146
Summerson, Rupert 11, 21–2, 24, 48, 67, 100, 104, 140, 146, 154, 160, 166, 193, 195, 214, *7, 18, 27, 116, 119*; cracked hands 155, 176; as deputy leader 23, 37–8, 48, 51, 66, *100*; experience 45, 172; frostbite 109, 116; as navigator 72, 209; personality 109, 172; scientific research programme 107, 109, 137, 162–3; twists ankle 207
Sumo wrestling 39
sun phetometer 163
survival: personality change in 126, 128; techniques 45, 79, 86–8, 102–4
Swan, Charles 213
Swan, Robert, *4, 23, 27, 75, 101, 111, 112, 115, 124*; back problems 53, 115, 122, 127, 150, 157, 164, 165, 176, 194; as explorer 35–7; as leader 38, 126; organises expedition 21–34; and sledges 52–3, 55

team spirit 38, 48, 54, 56, 69, 91–2, 116–17, 125–6, 160, 168; and arguments 51–3, 82, 125–6, 176–7
temperature, warmer 123–5, 132, 156, 162, 200
tent fires 39, 85, 107
tent life 77–8, 82–3, 84–5
tent slippers 136
tents 39, 77; erecting 39, 142, *19*
Tessa, student 180
Thatcher, Prime Minister Margaret 63, 216
thin ice 152–4, 182
thresholds, exhaustion and pain 95, 145
tidal fluctuations 89
Tolson, John 66, 72, 106–7, 130
Tomomi, student, 150
Toulouse, France 50–1, 197

tracking service 51
training 28, 34–56, 149, *20*
Twin Otters 17, 146, 169, *34, 37*; diffi-
    culties 130; grounded 129, 130; pilots,
    skill 198–9; resupply by 102, 105–7

United Nations 63; flag 92, 213

vagueness, following exhaustion 187
Van Andel, Jay 29–30
vapour barrier bags 48, 85, 103
Vatnajokull icecap, Iceland 21
Vikings, and ravens 50
visibility low 127–8, 152, 156

Walkmans, use of 164
Ward Hunt Island 64, 68

warmth, increasing 123–5, 132, 156, 162,
    200
water, open 162, 176, 200, *72, 73*; cross-
    ing 169–71; as danger signal 123, 128
water, problems with 102–4
'water sky' 192
Wendy, student 149
West Germany 129
Weypracht, Karl 136
white-out 152
Williams, Stephen 50, 62–3, 68, 102,
    118, *29, 105*
windchill factor 86
Wood, Gareth 12, 15, 16, 17, 18, 21, 157
working day, length of 138 176, 196

Yomiuri Shimbun 27, 67–8, 150
youth, and environmental issues 19